THIRTEEN

THIRTEEN

A Teenage Guide to Judaism

by

MORRIS MANDEL

illustrated by

LIL GOLDSTEIN

JONATHAN DAVID · *Publishers* Inc.
New York, N. Y.

© Copyright 1961
by
JONATHAN DAVID · Publishers, Inc.
131 East 23 Street, New York 10, N. Y.

Printed in U.S.A. by
NOBLE OFFSET PRINTERS, INC.
NEW YORK 3, N. Y.

To the Sacred Memory of My Father-in-Law
HARRY ROTH

THIRTEEN

is Humbly Dedicated

"Could we with ink the ocean fill,
  Were every blade of grass a quill,
  Were the world, of parchment made,
  And every man a scribe by trade;
        To write the love
        Of God above,
  Would drain the ocean dry;
        Nor would the scroll
        Contain the whole,
  Though stretched from sky to sky . . ."
                              Meir B. Isaac Nehorai

TABLE
OF CONTENTS

PREFACE

As in America, educators in Israel are becoming increasingly concerned about the state of Jewish *consciousness* or Jewish *awareness*. This concern is expressed by a newly coined expression: *toda-a yehudit*. A definite yearning exists, in Israel as it does in America, which aims at bringing to the uninitiated younger generation a comprehensive knowledge of Jewish law and lore, through the oral and printed word, in a manner that is palatable and meaningful.

The tragic destruction of the great Jewish centers of learning in Europe makes it imperative that we acquaint the youth of today, both in America and Israel, with that very thing for which their ancestors gave their lives. So little of it is known to them.

The problem of presenting in a nutshell what takes a lifetime to study, is indeed most difficult. Many doubt the possibility of ever solving this problem, and like Shammai of old, they resent anyone who would approach them with such a request. Others like Hillel of old, not only believe in a possible solution, but greatly sympathize with those who show even the slightest eagerness to know their past. For the latter, the problem is rather that of method: what to include, and how to present it, so that the student might develop an appetite for further study and investigation.

Rabbi Israel Salanter, who strongly recommended the introduction of ethical teaching in the curriculum of Jewish higher schools of learning, was once asked what he would advise for a student who can spend only one hour a day for Jewish studies—should he devote it to the study of Talmud or ethics? His answer was: devote it to the study of ethics, and then you will find many more hours for the study of Talmud.

The aim of *Thirteen* is to give its young reader a taste of the great Jewish heritage, so that he will become interested in studying it from its sources and thus deepen and widen his knowledge of it.

The author of *Thirteen*, Dr. Morris Mandel, principal of the English Department of one of the largest and finest Jewish Day Schools in Brooklyn, New York, has made a valuable contribution by popularizing our literature so that it might lead to a "functioning Judaism." Written in the year which marks the thirteenth anniversary of the State of Israel, *Thirteen* is a welcome addition to the teen-age literature of our day. It will serve as an invaluable aid in resolving the problem facing the Jewish educator of America and Israel alike—that of making our youth more aware and more conscious of Judaism—*toda-a*.

From time to time we are confronted by a lost generation. Here and there educators complain as did Joseph's brothers: "We have a father, an old man, and a child of his old age, a little one; and his brother is dead" (Genesis 44:20). But here and there the supposedly dead brother announces that he is alive!

We are confident that the young generation will come to life again!

SAMUEL K. MIRSKY, Ph.D.

Rabbi, Young Israel Synagogue
of Borough Park
Professor of Rabbinics,
Yeshiva University

PROLOGUE

A school principal was asked: "Where in your curriculum do you teach religion?"

Without hesitation, he replied, "We teach it all day long. We teach it in the arithmetic class by accuracy. We teach it in our English courses by learning to say what we really mean. In history there is the emphasis on honesty; in science on the development of breadth of mind. In crafts we teach thoroughness; in astronomy we teach reverence. We teach it in recreation by fair play. We teach it by courtesy, cooperation and understanding, not only by precept but by example. The young are learning that we, their elders, are anxious to help, guide, encourage and point out the way.

Judaism aims to be a living religion. It teaches that the torch of religion may be lit in the synagogue but must continue to burn in home and office; in the factory and on the street.

In Ecclesiastes, it is written: "Of making many books there is no end." Yet, THIRTEEN, is not just another book. It aims to strengthen the bonds of Judaism by deepening the love for its traditions, teaching an appreciation of the richness of its beliefs, stressing the observance of its tenets. To be an adult Jew means to know and preserve great spiritual treasures, to live by the rules of civil conduct prescribed by our prophets and rabbis, by the psalmist, lawgiver, and sage, and to walk humbly in the presence of both God and man. To be an adult Jew means to be a true disciple of the Torah, a lover of mankind and a sincere worshipper of God, for this is why the Jew was created.

The validity of any religion is tested by its effect on human conduct. Judaism promotes the good life, cleanses the mind from error, the heart from hatred, and conduct from sin. It awakens within a desire to do justly, love mercy, and walk humbly with God.

A wise man once said:

> A religion
> That costs nothing,
> That suffers nothing,
> Is worth nothing.

It is my sincere prayer that this volume may prove helpful to our teen-agers; that it may motivate Jewish youth to a more intense religious awareness and practice.

The main object of Judaism is not to get a man into heaven but to get heaven into man.

I wish to record my gratitude to those who have made this volume possible. My deep appreciation to my dear mother and father, Rebecca and Max Mandel, great protagonists of orthodox Judaism, who instilled in my life a deep love of religion. They planted their religious seeds deep in my heart.

I also wish to express my thanks to Rabbi Alfred J. Kolatch for his friendly and practical guidance, and to my friend Rabbi Nathan Ehrlich for his help in proof-reading the final copy.

Morris Mandel

Brooklyn, New York

chapter 1

YOU ARE THIRTEEN

"We must ever be mindful that our behavior . . . determines the name and fame,
the fate and faith of Israel."

The Jewish Way of Life

"And thou shalt teach them diligently to thy children..."

DEUTERONOMY

YOU ARE THIRTEEN

Thirteen is an important number in Jewish history. Tradition tells us that Moses made thirteen copies of the Torah. Bezalel was thirteen when he was appointed to oversee construction of the Tabernacle. God is described by thirteen characteristics. Maimonides laid down Thirteen Principles of Faith. There were thirteen horn-shaped collecting boxes, thirteen tables and thirteen devotional bowings in the Temple service. There are thirteen covenants written about circumcision. Rabbi Ishmael says Jewish law is to be expounded according to thirteen logical rules.

For you personally, thirteen is important because it marks the age when you are charged with living according to that law, the age when you are asked to carry forward the principles and practices of Judaism, the age of your religious maturity. To put it another way, thirteen marks the beginning of your responsibility to help keep alive the miracle—the miracle that is the unique survival of the Jewish people over the centuries in the face of unequaled persecution, suffering and wandering. As the famous Jewish philosopher, Martin Buber, points out: "The past of his (the Jew's) people is his personal memory; the future of his people is his personal task; the way of his people teaches him to will and understand his true self."

But who are these "people?" What is a Jew? What are you? Some of the answers to these questions have been provided in simple yet eloquent terms by the great Russian writer Leo Tolstoy:

16

"The Jew is that sacred being who brought down from Heaven the everlasting fire, and has illumined with it the entire world. He is the religious source, spring and fountain out of which all the rest of the peoples have drawn their beliefs and their religions.

"The Jew is the pioneer of liberty. Even in those olden days, when the people were divided into but two distinct classes, slaves and masters—even so long ago, the law of Moses prohibited the practice of keeping a person in bondage for more than six years.

"The Jew is the pioneer of civilization. Ignorance was condemned in olden Palestine more even than it is today in civilized Europe . . .

"The Jew is the emblem of eternity. He who neither slaughter nor torture of thousands of years could destroy, he who neither fire nor sword nor inquisition was able to wipe off from the face of the earth, he who was the first to produce the oracles of God, he who has been for so long the guardian of prophecy, and who transmitted it to the rest of the world . . . such a nation cannot be destroyed. The Jew is everlasting as is eternity itself."

This seeming indestructibility, however, is not some special reward which God continues to give the Jew for his having served as messenger of the world's moral and religious teachings. On the contrary, a study of the past reveals that it was achieved through certain positive actions of the Jewish people themselves, and it is important that we know what these were because they are the keys to our future as well. The American writer Will Durant points to them when, while marvelling at the courage of the Jew, he writes in his book *The Story of Philosophy*:

"The story of the Jews since the Dispersion is one of the epics of European history. Driven from their natural home by the Roman capture of Jerusalem, and scattered by flight and trade among all the nations and to all the continents; persecuted and decimated by the adherents of the great religions—Christianity and Mohammedanism—which had been born of their scriptures and their memories; barred by the feudal system from owning land, and by the guilds from taking part in industry; shut up within congested ghettos and narrowing pursuits, mobbed by the people and robbed by the Kings; building with their finance

17

and trade the towns and cities indispensable to civilization; outcast and excommunicated, insulted and injured; yet without any
political structure, without any legal compulsion to social unity,
without even a common language, *this wonderful people has
maintained itself in body and soul, has preserved its racial and
cultural integrity, has guarded with jealous love its oldest rituals
and traditions, has patiently and resolutely awaited the day of
its deliverance*, and has emerged greater in number than ever
before, renowned in every field for the contributions of its
geniuses, and triumphantly restored, after two thousand years of
wandering, to its ancient and unforgotten home. What drama
could rival the grandeur of these sufferings, the variety of these
scenes, and the glory and justice of this fufillment? What fiction
could match the romance of this reality?"

To which one might respond by spelling out the lesson that
is apparent in the above with the words of the American Jewish
philosopher Abraham J. Heschel:

"We are God's stake in human history. We are the dawn and
the dusk, the challenge and the test. . . . We have been offered
as a pattern of worship and as a prey for scorn, but there is still
more in our destiny. We carry the gold of God in our souls to
forge the gate of the kingdom. The time for the kingdom may
be far off, but the task is plain: to retain our share in God in spite
of peril and contempt."

Other writers have been moved to compare Judaism to
water, because it cleanses men of what is animal and low; to
wine, because time cannot injure it; to oil, because it does not
mix freely with foreign elements; to honey, because it is sweet
and lovely; to a wall, because it protects its followers from the
violence of the wicked; to manna, because it proclaims human
equality before God; to a vine, which is trodden under foot, because later its wine is placed on the king's table; and lastly to a
crown, because it invests man with sovereignty and raises him
higher than nature.

Indeed, Judaism is not simply a religion. It is a culture, a
civilization, a complete way of life. It has its own language,
literature, ethical values and aspirations. Its institutions are the
family, the school, the synagogue, and society in general. Its aims

are social justice and individual perfection. Its eternal goal is a better world—and toward this end it has made, and continues to make, inestimable contributions to the entire community of man.

Society, of course, also has benefited from the efforts of different civilizations. Yet, as Mark Twain so aptly put it:

"The Egyptian, the Babylonian, and the Persian rose, filled the planet with sound and splendor, than faded to dream stuff and passed away; the Greek and Roman followed and made a vast noise, and they are gone; other peoples have sprung up and held their torch high for a time, but it burned out, and they sit in twilight now, or have vanished. The Jew saw them all, beat them all, and is now what he always was, exhibiting no decadence, no infirmities of age, no weakening of his parts, no slowing of his energies, and no dulling of his alert and aggressive mind.

"If the statistics are right," Twain also observed, "the Jews constitute but one percent of the human race. It suggests a nebulous dim puff of star dust lost in the blaze of the Milky Way. Properly, the Jew ought hardly to be heard of; but he is heard of, has always been heard of. He has made a marvelous fight in this world, in all ages, and he has done it with his hands tied behind him."

Consider for a moment the long and glorious record that inspired Twain. Abraham spreading the word of God and remaining loyal in his lonely vigil . . . Isaac teaching spiritual living to his family . . . Jacob wrestling with the angel . . . Joseph portraying loyalty and patriotism to an adopted country . . . Moses giving Rameses an object lesson in human rights . . . Mordecai teaching Haman that no human being should bow to another.

On the battlefield, the Jew exhibited his bravery under the Maccabees. His courage in the campaign which ended with Titus' destruction of Jerusalem, his desperate rebellion under Bar Kochba, his defense of Naples against Balisarius, his determined courage in the bloody Warsaw rebellion against the barbaric might of the mechanized Nazi Army—all stand out as remarkable examples to mankind of a people's unwillingness to compromise its beliefs even in the face of death.

19

On the various roads to human progress, the Jew can trace his footsteps through the ages. "We are largely indebted to the Jews," wrote Santos, "for our first knowledge of philosophy, botany, medicine, astronomy, cosmography, not less than for the elements of grammar, the sacred languages, and almost all branches of biblical study."

Ancient Hebrew literature is replete with all phases of medical knowledge. Detailed descriptions of many parts of the body are given in the Talmud; the use of antitoxins derived from infected animals was advocated by Rabbi Ishmael centuries ago.

The Jew's attitude toward the empirical search for wisdom, which accounts for his advances in these and other areas, is reflected in the following excerpt from the "Physician's Prayer," attributed to the great, 12th century rabbi-philosopher-physician Moses Maimonides:

> If physicians more learned than I wish to counsel me, inspire me, O God, with confidence in, and obedience toward, the recognition of them—for the study of science is great. It is not given to one alone to see all that others see. May I be moderate in everything, except in the knowledge of this science. . . . Grant me the strength and opportunity always to correct what I have acquired, always to extend its domain; for knowledge is boundless, and the spirit of man can also extend infinitely and enrich itself daily with new acquisitions.

In the light of this attitude, it is not surprising that a Jew, Louis de Santangel, financed Columbus' first voyage to the New World with a loan of 17,000 florins. And when Columbus sighted land he sent Luis de Torres, a Jew, to scout the country. De Torres was the first white man to settle in Cuba.

As one who knocked at the gates of Peter Stuyvesant's New Amsterdam only thirty-five years after the Pilgrim Fathers stepped ashore on Plymouth Rock, the Jew also ranks among the trail blazers in the United States. He has tilled the soil on the farm and helped establish professions in the city; he has labored in the mine, the mill, the factory. In the Revolutionary War, Jewish soldiers fought in Washington's ragged armies and Jewish merchants, under the leadership of Haym Solomon, raised funds to assist in financing this struggle for liberation. Later, Jews participated in John Brown's revolt against slavery, and thousands of Jews served in the ranks of the Union and Confederate armies in the Civil War.

In this century, Jews have patriotically given their lives for their country in World War I, World War II and the Korean War. Jewish bodies are found in heroes' graves in Arlington National Cemetery. It was in truth that the historian William Lecky said: "Hebraic mortar cemented the foundations of American democracy."

It is on the level of social justice, however, that the Jew has made one of his most important contributions to his fellow man. For at the core of his tradition is the doctrine that God created man in His image, that all men are His equal children, and that each possesses within him a spark of the Divine which may not be violated. Thus the Jew is taught:

> "Thou shalt not oppress thy neighbor nor rob him; the wages of a hired servant shall not abide with thee all night until the morning. Thou shalt not curse the deaf, nor put a stumbling block before the blind, but thou shalt fear thy God, I am the Lord."

"Why," ask the Rabbis, "is the word justice written twice in the Bible ('Justice, justice shalt thou pursue.')? To teach us that we must practice justice at all times, whether it be for our profit or for our loss, and toward all men—toward Jews and non-Jews alike!" This democratic ideal, the constantly recurring theme in our literature, has been studied by great men of all nations. They have borrowed freely from its depth, its beauty and its wisdom.

Maxim Gorky, one of the great Russian novelists wrote: "In my early youth, I read—I have forgotten where—the words of the ancient Jewish sage—Hillel, if I remember rightly: 'If thou art not for thyself, who will be for thee? But if thou art for thyself alone, wherefore art thou?'

"The inner meaning of these words impressed me with its profound wisdom, and I interpreted them for myself in this manner: I must actively take care of myself, that my life should be better, and I must not impose the care of myself on other people's shoulders; but if I am going to take care of myself alone, of nothing but my own personal life, it will be useless, ugly, meaningless. This thought ate its way deep into my soul, and I say now with conviction: Hillel's wisdom served as a strong staff on my road, which was neither even nor easy. I believe that Jewish wisdom is more all-human and universal than any other; and this not only because of its immemorial age, not only because it is the first-born, but also because of the powerful humaneness that saturates it, because of its high estimate of man."

The American clergyman and editor, Lyman Abbott, concurred and went still further: "The world owes a debt to Israel; we Gentiles owe our life to Israel. It is Israel who has brought us the message that God is One, and that God is a just and righteous God, and demands righteousness of His children and nothing else. It is Israel who has brought us the message that God is our father. It is Israel who, in bringing us the divine law, has laid the foundation of liberty. It is Israel who had the first free institutions the world ever saw. It is Israel who has brought us our Bible, our Prophets. When some time our own un-Christian prejudices flame out against the Jewish people, let us remember that all that we have and all that we are we owe, under God, to what Judaism has given us."

The testimony is clear, the record is unchallengeable. Now that you are thirteen, now that there is new meaning to your words when you say, "I am a Jew," you might do well to remember the story of the man who went to the Museum of Art. He looked at a masterpiece for a long time and then declared to the attendant, "I can't, for the life of me, see why this picture is so famous!"

"Sir," explained the attendant, "this picture is not on trial any longer. You are."

Judaism has stood the test of time, it is no longer on trial. But you, the new religious adult, are.

chapter 2

THE BAR MITZVAH

"Save me from temptation, so that I may
observe Thy holy Law and those precepts
on which human happiness and eternal
life depend."

Benjamin Artom

THE BAR MITZVAH

Literally, Bar Mitzvah means "a son of the Commandment." And whether you win or lose your trial, whether you melt into the masses or become part of the eternal masterpiece that is Judaism, depends upon your living according to the laws and traditions that distinguish the Jew and preserve his identity. Moreover, the strength of your case, the extent to which you enrich your daily life by following God's commandments, now rests entirely in your hands.

For you are in somewhat the same position as the contractor who worked for a large construction corporation for many years and one day was given plans to build a luxurious model home in a very exclusive residential section. The board of directors instructed him to spare no expense.

As the work progressed, the contractor thought to himself: "Who will be the wiser if I don't use the most expensive materials and the best labor? Outwardly, the house will look the same." He began to substitute cheap materials and labor, pocketing the difference.

Shortly after the house was finished, the Chairman of the Board held a reception to celebrate its completion. He made a lengthy speech and then surprised the contractor by presenting him with the keys and the deed to the house. "We give you this," the chairman said, "as a token of our high esteem for your many years of splendid and faithful service."

In the years that followed, the contractor never ceased to regret the way he had cheated himself. "If only I had known," he would murmur, "that I was building this house for myself."

As a Bar Mitzvah, you were called to say the blessings at the Torah and you proclaimed your adherence to its teachings; you made your contract with the Almighty and became responsible for your future. Unlike the man in our story, you know for whom you are building; you know that you will be the biggest loser if you don't fulfill your obligations to the best of your ability. Bear in mind that when God takes the measure of man He puts the tape around the heart, not the head or the bankroll; He is concerned with how many people you have willingly helped, how many friendships you have made, how many institutions you have supported as a full partner in the construction of His universe.

Remember, too, that as a Bar Mitzvah it is both your privilege and duty to perform various religious functions. One of the most familiar, of course, is the daily putting on of the *tefillin*. This makes you stop each morning, amid the mad dash toward worldly pursuits, to recall your relationship to God. This is a "sign on your hand" and a "memorial between your eyes," which daily reminds you that you are a Jew. If you are too rushed to put on your *tefillin*, if you find yourself forgetting them, chances are that you are too rushed to give much thought to your role on this earth as a Jew; that you are forgetting your heritage and melting into the masses. For the *mitzvah* of *tefillin*, like all our religious practices, embodies two basic characteristics: it draws us to God, and it preserves our identity.

The *tefillin* and the *talit* (prayer shawl) are put on each weekday morning; on Sabbath and Festivals, only the *talit* is worn. This is because we read in the book of Exodus: "And it (the *tefillin*) shall be a sign unto thee: for a sign upon thine hand, and for a memorial between thine eyes, in order that the Law of the Lord shall be in thy mouth." The sign is not needed on the Sabbath and Festivals, since these holy days are in themselves a sign between God and Israel.

One must be careful not to desecrate the holiness of the *tefillin*. As Rabbi Bibi warned, "Take not the name of the Lord in

27

vain. Do not wear *tefillin* and then go out transgressing with the Divine name on thy forehead." The *tefillin* are bound first around the arm and then around the brow. They contain four sections of Scripture:

1. "Hear, O Israel . . ." This teaches the unity of God, that God is one; that we must love God with all our heart, with all our soul, with all our strength; that this love of God must govern our actions, our words, our thoughts; that wherever we go and whatever we do, we must think of God's presence and of His might.

2. "And it shall be when the Lord shall bring thee into the Land . . ." This turns our minds toward the land of Israel. It promises the Holy Land as a dwelling for the Jewish people and stresses what possession of the Holy Land means: the establishment of a center of light and religion not for the Jew alone but for the whole human race.

3. "And it shall come to pass . . ." This teaches us that the Lord is a God of Justice, that He deals with men according to their merits. No good action goes unrewarded, and evil will sooner or later meet with its deserved punishment.

4. "Sanctify unto me all the first-born . . ." This teaches the all-important lesson that our people have been chosen by God as a nation consecrated to His service, that they must be a holy people and lead pure and righteous lives.

No less than by the *tefillin*, your new role in the Jewish scheme of things is clearly illustrated by the fact that you are now counted for the *minyan*, the quorum of ten men which is required before a congregation can start services. This is pointed up in a very revealing story by Rabbi Alfred J. Kolatch.

WAITING FOR TEN

Jack Kline wasn't always Ten. When he was five he wasn't Ten and when he was fifteen he wasn't Ten. Nor was he Ten when he was ten. He was almost thirty before he became Ten, and then only through repeated coincidences that seemed almost to form a pattern.

Jack loved to recall his past, especially now that he was on the road for months at a time trying to sell Southern shopkeepers the latest New York styles in dresses. The thoughts of his early youth at home brought him moments of pleasure. Lying on his bed on a Friday night in quiet, one-hotel towns like South Hill, Virginia, or Carrollton, Georgia, the picture of mother with head covered, lighting candles, or dad with cup of wine in hand chanting the age-old *kiddush,* as the family looked on, would cause a tear to well up in the corner of his eye. Prolonged thought frequently would swell the tear, forcing it over the lid.

In his youth Jack followed his father to *Shul* on Friday or Saturday, at first willingly, later reluctantly. He recalled the routine reminders, then urgings, then threats which preceded each pilgrimage. But he always went.

He wasn't sorry now. It had been torture, but the misery had turned into comfort. In his travels to many strange cities and towns he would often forget his customers on a Sabbath morning and seek out the synagogue. Frequently his search met with failure. At times, however, his search was successful, and in the warm handshake and cordial greeting that he received he found recompense for the days of his youth in which the losing battle against enforced synagogue attendance was waged. So it was that the series of coincidences developed which made Jack Kline Ten when he was almost thirty.

For invariably, as Jack approached the house of worship in the smaller communities, he would find that the service had not begun. In the winter months, men would be huddled around a radiator off to the side or around a pot-bellied oil or gas burner in the rear. In the warmer weather, they would be standing on the threshold or sitting on the stoop enjoying a cool breeze.

"What's up," Jack would say. Always the answer would be "waiting for a *minyan*," or "waiting for Ten."

More often than not Jack would be "Ten" and the service would begin, to the great relief of the nine who had almost given up hope of a service. The thought of having saved the day thrilled Jack. And the thought of appearing so often when "nine" were "waiting for Ten" pleased him greatly. It gave him a feeling of importance.

Without him there could be no service. "I'm Ten," he often thought of himself. "Without Ten there can be no service."

And all over the country, in the smaller communities where Jews congregate to pray, people are waiting for Ten.

Besides such tangible practices as putting on *tefillin* or being part of a *minyan*, Judaism has a less tangible but not less important side that also requires your observance. Actually, Judaism is a system of spiritual truths, moral laws and religious practices. The moral laws and religious practices have been duly classified, codified, and clothed with binding authority; the more elusive spiritual doctrines are largely uncharted. As a result, some people mistakenly believe that in Judaism "religion means not creed but a way of life." What they fail to realize is that "a way of life without guiding principles and thoughts is not worth living." Maimonides set down what he considered to be some of the fundamental doctrines of Judaism in his "Thirteen Principles of the Faith," which has been made part of the daily service.

THIRTEEN PRINCIPLES OF THE FAITH

1. I believe with perfect faith that the Creator, blessed be His Name, is the Author and Guide of everything that has been created, and that He alone has made, does make, and will make all things.
2. I believe with perfect faith that the Creator, blessed be His name, is a Unity, and that there is no unity in any manner like unto His, and that He alone is our God, who was, is, and will be.

30

3. I believe with perfect faith that the Creator, blessed be His Name, is not a body, and that He is free from all the properties of matter, and that He has not any form whatsoever.

4. I believe with perfect faith that the Creator, blessed be His Name, is the first and last.

5. I believe with perfect faith that to the Creator, blessed be His Name, and to Him alone, it is right to pray, and that it is not right to pray to any being besides Him.

6. I believe with perfect faith that all the words of the Prophets are true.

7. I believe with perfect faith that the prophecy of Moses our teacher, peace be unto him, was true, and that he was the chief of the Prophets, both of those that preceded and of those that followed.

8. I believe with perfect faith that the whole Torah, now in our possession, is the same that was given to Moses, our teacher, peace be unto him.

9. I believe with perfect faith that this Torah will not be changed, and that there will never be any other from the Creator, blessed be His Name.

10. I believe with perfect faith that the Creator, blessed be His Name, knows every deed of the children of men, and all their thoughts, as it is said, 'It is He that fashioneth the hearts of them all, that giveth heed to all their works.'

11. I believe with perfect faith that the Creator, blessed be His Name, rewards those that keep His commandments, and punishes those that transgress them.

12. I believe with perfect faith in the coming of the Messiah; and, though He tarry, I will wait for His coming.

13. I believe with perfect faith that there will be a revival of the dead at the time when it shall please the Creator, blessed be His Name, and exalted be His fame for ever and ever.

For Thy salvation I hope, O Lord!

If you believe in the Lord, He will do half your work—but the last half. God helps those who help themselves. As a rabbi once explained to his congregation: "In the Kingdom of God there is always an election going on. Only three votes are cast. The Lord always votes for you. Satan always votes against you. And you have the deciding vote."

To guide you in casting that "deciding vote," our vast literature points out the path of wisdom: "Who is a wise man? He who learns from every one capable to instruct him. Who is a strong man? He who controls his passions. Who is the rich man? He who knows how to enjoy his portion in life; he is happy in this life, and blessed in the life to come. Who is the honored man? He who honors his fellow men."

And in the "Ethics of the Fathers" we read: "There are seven marks of an uncultured man, and seven of a wise man. The wise man does not speak before him who is greater than he in wisdom, and does not break in upon the speech of his fellow; he is not hasty to answer; he questions according to the subject matter, and answers to the point; he addresses himself to first things first and to the last last; regarding that which he has not understood he says, 'I do not understand it,' and acknowledges the truth."

At thirteen, as you draw the plans that will shape the practical course of your new life, try to build upon the following foundation:

1. The love of God
2. The value of time
3. The success of perseverance
4. The pleasure of working
5. The dignity of simplicity
6. The worth of character
7. The power of kindness
8. The influence of example
9. The wisdom of economy
10. The virtue of patience
11. The development of talent
12. The obligation of duty
13. The joy of originating

Finally, now that you are a Bar Mitzvah, now that you are faced with meeting the test of your trial as a Jew, this prayer, which was written by Benjamin Artom in 1686, and is still used in Sephardic synagogues throughout the world, should serve as a testimony of your faith:

"O my God, and God of My Fathers:

"On this solemn and sacred day, which marketh my passage from boyhood to manhood, I humbly raise my eyes to Thee, and declare with sincerity and truth that henceforth I will observe all Thy Commandments, and undertake to bear the responsibility of all mine actions toward Thee. In my earliest infancy I was brought within Thy sacred covenant with Israel and today I again enter as an active responsible member the pale of Thine elect congregation, in the midst of which I will never cease to glorify Thy holy Name in the face of all nations. Do Thou, O heavenly Father, hearken unto this my humble prayer, and bestow upon me Thy gracious blessings, so that my earthly life may be sustained and made happy by Thine ineffable mercies. Teach me the way of Thy statute, that I may obey them, and faithfully carry out Thy ordinances. Dispose my heart to love Thee and to fear Thy holy Name, and grant me Thy support and the strength necessary to avoid the worldly dangers which beset the path lying before me. Save me from temptation, so that I

may observe Thy holy Law and those precepts on which human happiness and eternal life depend. Thus I will every day of my life trustfully and gladly proclaim:

"Hear, O Israel, The Lord Is Our God, The Lord Is One!"

chapter 3

DAUGHTERS IN ISRAEL

"A woman's wisdom buildeth her house."
Proverbs 14:1

"A woman of valor
who can find?
She is more precious
than rubies."

PROVERBS

DAUGHTERS IN ISRAEL

According to tradition, the female age of religious maturity actually is twelve, although in this country the tendency among Conservative and Reform groups is to celebrate it at thirteen. The important thing, however, is that as a daughter in Israel you are also on trial, you are also at the point where the extent of your adherence to the laws and practices of your religion will determine whether you melt into the masses or become part of the eternal masterpiece that is Judaism.

In some ways, in fact, your responsibility is heavier than that of your male counterpart. For tradition entrusts to the woman, the wife and mother, not only the keeping of the home but the rearing and educating of the children. "Listen," the child is told, "to the counsel of your father and the Torah teachings of your mother." So you play a dual role in the life-drama of your people. The preservation and perpetuation of Judaism depends both on your own observances and on your communicating their beauty and age-old meaning to your family.

The significance attached to this dual role can be seen in the special conditions designed to assist you in its performance. The woman, like the man, must observe all prohibitions, all "thou shalt nots." But because the woman has the obligation of running the home, raising the children, creating the atmosphere of *Shabbat* and *Yom Tov*, she is excused from performing the affirmative

38

precepts, or the "thou shalt" commandments that must be performed at a definite time. Thus, since *tefillin* are put on only at the time of morning prayer, the woman is excused. Similarly, the woman is not required to eat in the *Succah*, or hear the blowing of the *shofar*.

However, the woman's obligations include giving charity, saying the Grace after meals, participating in the *Chanukah* candle lighting ceremony, and listening to the reading of the *Purim Megillah*. Of course women who wish to observe the precepts limited to a specific time may do so. For example, all Jews regardless of sex, have always listened to the blowing of the *shofar* on the High Holy Days.

The value and importance of woman is stressed early in the Bible. As the story of the patriarchs unfolds, we also see the tremendous devotion and heroism of the matriarchs, the mothers of the Jewish nation.

First there is Sarah, the essence of beauty and virtue. She worked side by side with her saintly husband, Abraham, helping him spread God's teachings among a pagan people.

Then there is Rebecca. Tradition tells us that as long as Sarah lived a cloud hung over her tent; when she died that cloud disappeared. When Rebecca came it returned. As long as Sarah lived her doors were wide open; when she died that hospitality ceased. When Rebecca came it returned. As long as Sarah lived there was a blessing on her bread, and the lamp in her tent burned from Sabbath eve to Sabbath eve; when she died these ceased. When Rebecca came the blessings returned. "Isaac brought her into the tent of Mother Sarah, and Rebecca became his wife," for he saw in her the beauty and idealism characteristic of his mother.

Next there is Rachel. Have you ever read a story which equalled in genuine beauty the deep, unselfish love of Jacob for Rachel? He worked for fourteen years to earn her hand in marriage. The prophet Jeremiah declares that Rachel is buried in a grave on the road to Ephrat so that she can be on hand to entreat the Lord to show her children mercy. Rachel weeps from her grave, refusing to be comforted, as long as her children are strangers in foreign countries. And Jeremiah envisions Rachel

rising from her grave to hear God's soothing words: "Thus saith the Lord: Refrain thy voice from weeping, and thine eyes from tears; for thy work shall be rewarded, and they shall come back again from the land of the enemy."

"God has endowed women with a special sense of wisdom which man lacks," states the Talmud. "Woman determines man's behavior," the sages further advise. To illustrate, they tell of a pious couple who lived together for ten years and, having no children, were divorced. The man married an impious woman and she transformed him into a man of wickedness. The pious woman married a man of wickedness and she transformed him into a man of goodness.

The Bible describes God as creating woman for the very purpose of marriage. "And the Lord God said, 'it is not good that the man should be alone; I will make him a help mate for him.'" A talmudic passage declares: "He who has no wife lacks joy, blessing and even life itself, and life without those things is not really life."

Interestingly, there is no Hebrew word for "marriage"; the word used is *kiddushin*, which means "holiness." For the relationship of man and woman in marriage is considered not merely a biological union, nor simply an economic partnership, but rather a sacred union under God.

Just as marriage is called *kiddushin*, the Jewish home is called a *mikdosh m'at*, "a little sanctuary." The home, as the dwelling place of God, is sacred: the husband is high priest, the wife high priestess.

This concept of marriage and home reaches its climax in motherhood. In Exodus we read: "Thus shalt thou say to the House of Jacob, and tell the children of Israel." "House of Jacob" here refers to the mothers, so Moses was told to first speak to them when the Torah was given to us. Why? Because it is the mother who teaches the child the fear of sin and the love of God, the ways of the past and the path of the future. Perhaps the strongest indication of Judaism's attitude toward mothers is the fact that the Fifth Commandment, which includes the charge to "honor thy mother," is placed right after the injunction hallowing the Sabbath.

One might draw the following word-portrait of a mother:

From the dependency of infancy to the dignity of maturity, children are under your influence. Very often the first word a child utters is "mother."

You come in different sizes, enjoy many things, share varied interests. You are found in every country in the world, and there is more than rumor to indicate that you inhabit God's celestial domain. Though you speak different languages, you are united in one goal: to help each child reach the highest degree of individual development.

You are a composite person. You have the energy of Samson, the efficiency of Joseph, the memory of Rashi, the understanding of Aaron, the wisdom of Solomon, the kindness of David, the patience of Job, the modesty of Moses, the nerves of Daniel, the warmth of Sarah, the loyalty of Rebecca, the devotion of Rachel, the love of Leah, the faith of Hannah, and the courage of Esther.

You are an inspiration to poets, a model for artists, the prayer of soldiers, God's messenger to children. To the writer you are the theme, to the philosopher the ideal, to the world the symbol of goodness.

You defied Pharoah, defeated Haman, waged war against Sisera, sacrificed seven sons to God, lived in loneliness for twenty-four years so that your husband could learn Torah, and gave up wealth, security and position for Judaism.

You are the greatest influence in your home, the center and soul of your family. Your heart is the child's schoolroom. You represent love, security and understanding. You are a symbol of all that is right. You have beauty, skill and grace. There is no velvet so soft as your lap, no rose so lovely as your smile, no friendship so pure, so devoted.

You are the source of good deeds and thoughts, the core of spiritual endeavors, the confidante of all undertakings. You give help without becoming a crutch, direct your children without stifling their growth, give sympathy without smothering. You enjoy the satisfactions, the delights and the pleasures of childhood, yet at the same time understand the griefs, irritations, embarrassments and frustrations of the young.

41

The most amazing thing about you, the thing that makes you different from any person in the universe, is that you will not entertain the idea of changing jobs with anyone in the world. In fact, you are thankful to God for having entrusted His children to you. Only you are destined to be immortal. "For your sake," teaches the Talmud, "for the sake of the mothers who kept faith in God alive in the hearts of their children, was Israel delivered from Egypt." Is it any wonder that Solomon proclaimed in Proverbs:

> You stretch out your hand to the poor; yea, you
> reach forth your hands to the needy.
> Strength and dignity are your clothing; and you
> laugh at the time to come.
> You open your mouth with wisdom; and the law of
> kindness is on your tongue.
> You look well to the ways of your household, and eat
> not the bread of idleness.
> Your children rise up, and call you blessed; your
> husband also praises you.
> Many daughters have done valiantly, but you
> excel them all.

Irene R. Wolf, in an article for the Jewish Library, second series, wrote the following about the Jewish mother as "The Priestess Of The Home:"

"How simply the *Shema* sums up the whole duty of man. In the opening sentence it defines our belief: The Lord is our God, and He is One. We must love Him and we must serve Him. How are we to do this? By learning from our parents what are our duties as laid down in the Torah, 'these words which I command thee.'

"Parents are to teach them diligently to their children at all times. This injunction is addressed to mothers as well as fathers. It is the mother who is with the child when he lies down and when he rises up; it is the mother who sits with him in the house and shows him, as well as tells him, how his life must be guided by fixed rules and principles. It is the mother who walks with

42

him and shows him the beauties of nature. Bringing a child to love nature quickly leads him to a greater love of nature's God, the Creator of heaven and earth. All this and much more is contained in the *Shema*. So with every prayer, there are meanings we all can find if we seek them.

"The carrying out of the laws of *kashrut*, of Sabbath holiness, and Holy Day observance are duties that fall naturally and almost exclusively into woman's sphere. Her systematic observance of these will make them a part of her very being. But she must be ready at all times to explain her reasons for carrying them out, for on her satisfactory answers to questions put by her children may depend their future adherence to these traditions. The curiosity and sentiment of childhood should be completely satisfied by the mother's explanation of the domestic symbols and ceremonies of Judaism. She is the one who can weave into the children's nature such a love and reverence for Judaism that it will permeate their lives, never to be lost. Gone is the age when children were content to ask no questions about religious observances, or were satisfied with the reply, 'I do this because my mother did it before me and her mother before her and we must carry on our customs without question.'

"Happily, Judaism stands as a pillar of enlightenment. It will withstand the onslaughts of doubt and questioning and rear its head above them all; the more we know of our religion the more we can revere it, for it appeals to the might of our reason as well as to our heart and to our soul.

"Great responsibility rests upon the woman for preserving the Sabbath spirit. There is no reason for the intrusion of worldly cares into the home on the Sabbath. Above all, Friday evening should be kept sacred, thus making for tranquility and happiness. The eve of the Sabbath is essentially a home evening, an evening devoted to family reunion; neither commercial interests nor social engagements nor frivolous amusements may interfere with its sanctity. The candles lighted by a loving mother, the priestess of the home; the parents' blessing of the children; the white tablecloth gleaming with the best dishes and savory food—what can replace the memory of these through life? What more precious moments are remembered from childhood than the candles of

43

Chanukah, the festivity of Purim, and the Seder table at Pesach? The man or woman who can look back upon such truly Jewish memories will have a bond with Judaism too strong to be broken by any passing influence or temptation. . . .

"A woman's deepest concern, the center of her affection, is her home. She should, however, have some outside work to which she gives attention. . . . Well advised is she who joins some study group or some charitable organization. There are so many ways in which a woman may find an outlet! The interest aroused in her children by her accounts of her activities may lead to an awakening also of an interest in communal affairs, for they may begin to feel their duty to the whole family of Israel. . . . Extensively, the interest of the home should be as broad as life itself; the essential work of the Jewish woman is to create and maintain that institution of unique purity and loveliness—the Jewish home."

The religious education of girls is therefore of special importance, since the Jewish daughter is the future mother of Israel; the person who builds the Jewish home, who educates the children, introduces the laws of *kashrut*, Sabbath observance, and holiday rituals. The Jewish woman must know what our religion demands of her before she can undertake that grave responsibility.

The Talmud reports the wise counsel given by a mother to a bride-to-be on how to build the Jewish home. "My daughter," she advised, "if you will respect your husband he will treat you like a queen. If you will serve him like a slave-girl, he will serve you like a slave. But if you will be too proud to serve him, he will treat you like a maid-servant. . . . If his friends come to his home, welcome them heartily. . . . Watch well your home and all your husband's possessions. He will be delighted with you and you will be the crown of his head."

To be sure, setting a firm foundation for a wholesome home life is not a one-sided affair. Displaying an uncanny understanding of the female and the manner in which she is to be treated, the Talmud says that a man should spend as much as he can afford on his wife's clothing.

And many thousands of years ago, in the year 1120, Judah ibn Tibbon, a physician, scholar and man of culture, counseled his son on marital happiness: "My son! I command thee to honor

44

thy wife to thine utmost capacity. She is intelligent and modest, a daughter of a distinguished and educated family. She is a good housewife and mother, and no spendthirft. Her tastes are simple, whether in food or dress. Remember her assiduous tendance of thee in thine illness, though she had been brought up in elegance and luxury. Remember how she afterwards reared thy son without man or woman to help her. Were she a hired nurse she would have earned thy esteem and forbearance; how much the more, since she is the wife of thy bosom, the daughter of the great, art thou bound to treat her with consideration and respect. To act otherwise is the way of the contemptible. . . . If thou wouldst acquire my love, honor her with all thy might; do not exercise too severe an authority over her; our Sages have expressly warned men against this. If thou givest orders or reprovest, let thy words be gentle. Enough is it if thy displeasure is visible in thy look, let it not be vented in actual rage."

Judah ibn Tibbon so ordered his son because he knew that Judaism's concept of marriage, home and motherhood is vital to our people's survival. He knew, too, as you must learn that it revolves around the woman, the wife and mother. He fully appreciated the burden which must be borne by the daughters of Israel, the strain of playing a dual role in a spectacular which might be called "The Life of Judaism."

When you find this too difficult, when you find yourself wondering whether you can meet the test of your trial, try to remember this poem:

> Be Strong!
> We are not here to play, to dream, to drift;
> We have hard work to do, and loads to lift;
> Shun not the struggle—face it; 'tis God's gift.
>
> Be Strong!
> Say not, "The days are evil. Who's to blame?"
> And fold the hands and acquiesce—oh shame!
> Stand up, speak out, and bravely, in God's name.

Be Strong!
It matters not how deep intrenched the wrong,
How hard the battle goes, the day how long;
Faint not—fight on! Tomorrow comes the song.

—*Anonymous*

chapter 4

THIS IS OUR GOD

"How do you know there is a God?" a small boy asked his friend, who was flying a kite so high that it was completely out of sight.

The lad looked up at the sky for a moment and replied: "In the same way that I know there is a kite up there—I feel the pull of it."

"This is my God and I will glorify Him. My father's God and I will extol Him."

EXODUS

THIS IS OUR GOD

Once, when the famous British surgeon, Lord Moyihan, had finished a delicate operation before a full gallery of distinguished visiting doctors, he was asked how he could work with such a large group present. "As far as I am concerned," he replied, "there are just three of us present in the operating room when I operate, the patient and myself."

"But that makes only two, who is the third?"

"The third is God," he said softly.

No doubt this answer came as something of a surprise to Lord Moyihan's questioner. The concept of one omnipresent, all-powerful God is not easy to grasp. It requires intense, unyielding belief that is the staff of Jewish life. It cannot be proven in the concrete way that, say, a mathematical equation can be proven. On the surface, it appears to defy the laws of logic. Yet it is the only logical explanation for all the wonders of heaven and earth that cannot otherwise be explained even in this space age.

How can we love God if we cannot see Him? If He is everywhere and knows everything, why do we have to seek Him out in prayer? The answer to these and the many other common questions concerning God is that each person's relationship to the Almighty is not only a deep but a highly personal expression of faith, and each person must act on the basis of that faith. One rabbi summed this up very simply and accurately: "Man finds God only where he seeks Him."

To those who are incapable of understanding this and still demand to see God as one man sees another, the following incident is especially interesting:

Emperor Trajan once said to Rabbi Joshua: "You teach that your God is everywhere and boast that He resides among your people. I should like to see Him."

"God's presence is indeed everywhere," replied Joshua, "but He cannot be seen; no mortal eye can behold His glory."

The Emperor insisted.

"A thousand pardons," said Joshua, "but if it please your Majesty, would you be good enough to first look at one of God's servants."

The Emperor thought for a moment and then agreed. So Joshua took him outside at noon and courteously asked him to look at the sun in all its splendor. "I cannot," said Trajan, "the light blinds me."

"If you are unable," observed Joshua, "to endure the light of one of His servants, how can you expect to behold the glory of the Creator?"

Actually, more often than not, those who demand to see God or to have incontrovertible evidence of His existence are merely looking for an excuse to avoid living according to His ordinances and serving Him. This brings up the question, how does one best serve God? Hundreds of years ago a pious scholar, Eliezer ben Isaac, spelled out the answer in a letter to his son:

"My son, give God all honor and the gratitude which is His due. Thou hast need of Him, but He needs thee not. Fear the Lord, the God of thy fathers. See that thou guardest thy soul's holiness, and when thou prayest, think well before whom it is thou standest. Visit the sick and suffering man, and let thy countenance be cheerful when he sees it, but not so that thou oppress the helpless one with gaiety. Respect the poor man by gifts whose hand he knows not of. Rather feed thyself with vilest weed than make thyself dependent on other human beings. Seek not greedily after power and pre-eminence in the world. Spend not thy time among people who speak ill of their brother man. Be not as the fly that is always seeking sick and

51

wounded places. Dare not to rejoice when thine enemy falls to the ground; give him food when he hungers. Purge thy soul from angry passion, that inheritance of fools. Love the society of wise men, and strive to know more and more of the ways and the works of thy Creator."

In our own time, Dr. Samuel Belkin, President of Yeshiva University, has observed that "For the Jew, the greatest way to serve God is to render service to man."

Perhaps no service that the Jewish people has performed for mankind equals its promulgation of the concept of one God, one Creator of the universe who is the Author of all life. The heart of Judaism has always been the *Shema*, "Hear, O Israel: The Lord Our God, The Lord Is One."

Abraham, the first hero of Jewish history, dedicated his life to spreading this truth. Our literature contains many stories that illustrate his deep faith in God, as you know from your Hebrew studies. But even if the story that follows is familiar to you, it is worth re-reading.

Terah, Abraham's father, was not only an idolator, but he manufactured idols and exhibited them for public sale. One day he had to go on an important mission and asked Abraham to take care of the shop. While Abraham reluctantly obeyed, he was determined to prove to his father that it was foolish to believe in man-made idols.

Along came an old man whose eye was caught by one of the idols on display. "What is the price of that god?" he asked.

"Old man," said Abraham, "may I be permitted to ask your age?"

"Three-score years," replied the idolator, somewhat taken aback by the question.

"Three-score years!" exclaimed Abraham, "and you would worship a thing that has been fashioned by the hands of my father's slaves within the past twenty-four hours? Strange that a man of sixty should be willing to bow his grey head to a creature of a day!"

The man, filled with shame, left hurriedly.

Soon after, a sedate matron entered the shop carrying a

large dish of flour in her hand. "Here," she said, "I have brought an offering to the gods. Place it before them and bid them be good to me."

"Place it before them yourself, foolish woman!" cried Abraham indignantly, "and see how greedily they will devour it."

She did so. Meanwhile, Abraham took a hammer and smashed the idols, except the largest, in whose hands he placed the instrument of destruction. When Terah returned, he was shocked at the sight that met his eyes.

"What is all this, Abraham! What wretch has dared defile our gods in this manner?"

"Why should I conceal anything from you father?" replied the pious son. "During your absence a woman came with an offering for the gods. She placed it before them. The younger gods had not tasted food for a long time. They greedily stretched forth their hands and began to eat before the old god had given them permission. Enraged at their boldness, he rose, took the hammer and punished them for their want of respect."

"Do you mock me? Will you deceive your aged father?" Terah raged. "Do I not know that they can neither eat, nor move?"

"And yet," rejoined Abraham, "you pay them divine honors and demand that I worship them!"

It was all in vain. He could not convince his father, who instead delivered him to the cruel tribunal of the idolatrous King Nimrod.

The tyrant urged Abraham to reconsider and worship the god of fire. "Your majesty," said Abraham, "would it not be wiser to worship water? It is mightier than fire having the power to extinguish it."

"Worship the water then," said Nimrod.

"Perhaps," reflected Abraham, "it would be more reasonable to worship the clouds which, by your own confession, are the source of much water and possess great power."

"But if power is to be the object of worship," continued Abraham, "then the preference should be given to the wind, for by its greater force it scatters the clouds."

"I see," said Nimrod, "we shall never be done with this prattler. Worship the wind then, and we will pardon your former profanations."

"Be not angry, great ruler," begged Abraham, "I cannot worship the fire, nor the water, nor the clouds, nor the wind, nor any of the things you call god. The power they possess is not their own. It is derived from a being more powerful and full of mercy and love. The Creator of heaven and earth, Him alone will I worship."

"Well then," snapped the tyrant, "since you refuse to worship the fire, you shall be made to feel its mighty force."

It was decreed that Abraham be thrown into a fiery furnace. But Nimrod was not to have his way, for God delivered Abraham from the raging flames and made him a source of blessing to many nations.

As you can see from the story of Abraham and the idols, Judaism preaches that there is only one God and that He is a living God.

We speak of the hands of God, the mouth of God, the eyes of God. Yet we believe that God is not a physical being and He is without physical organs. When we use such terms we mean them in a figurative sense only. But we do, nevertheless, see the power of God in the myriad of wonderful things all about us—the heavens, the stars, the growing plants and flowers; we see Him in each new-born child.

Job exclaims: "God thunders wondrously with His voice. He does great things which we cannot comprehend. For, to the snow He says: 'Fall on the earth!' and to the shower and the rain, 'Be strong.' He seals up the hands of every man, that all men may know His work. Then the beasts go into their lairs and remain in their dens. From its chamber comes the wild wind, and cold from the scattering winds. By the breath of God ice is given, and the broad waters are frozen fast. He loads the thick cloud with moisture; the clouds scatter His lightning. They turn round and round by His guidance, to accomplish all that He commands them on the face of the habitable world. Whether for correction, or for His land, or for love, He causes it to happen.

"God is He who giveth rain upon the earth, and sends waters upon the field. He sets up on high those that are lowly, and those who mourn are exalted to safety. He frustrates the devices of the crafty, so that their hands achieve no success. He takes the wise in their own craftiness, and schemes of the wily are brought to a quick end. They meet with darkness in the daytime, and grope at noonday as in the night. But He saves from the sword of their mouth; even the needy from the hand of the mighty. So the poor have hope, and iniquity shuts her mouth."

From God came all the glory of creation, all the beauty of nature, all the bounties of heaven and earth. To fully appreciate the blessing of life is to understand that everything you have is a gift from the Creator, and that every day of your life He renews His gift to you.

Tradition tells us that God revealed Himself to the Jews on Mount Sinai when He gave them His Torah. They had reached the Sinai desert and camped near the mountain on *Rosh Chodesh Sivan*, the first day of the third month after the exodus from Egypt. They had traveled under Divine protection for several months and daily had witnessed such miracles as the manna and the quail, sweetening of the water, the defeat of Amalek, and the crossing of the Red Sea. With each experience they became more conscious of God and their faith grew more intense.

Moses ascended Mount Sinai and God spoke to him: "Thus shalt thou say to the house of Jacob, and tell the children of Israel. You have seen what I did unto the Egyptians, and how I bore you on eagles' wings and brought you unto Myself. Now, therefore, if ye will hearken unto My voice, indeed, and keep My covenant, then ye shall be Mine own treasure from among all peoples; for all the earth is Mine; and ye shall be unto Me a Kingdom of priests and a holy nation."

Upon his return from Mount Sinai, Moses called together the elders of the people and put all these words of God before them. Unanimously, with one voice and one mind, the people answered: "Everything God has said, we shall do." Thus, they

accepted the Torah unconditionally, with all its precepts, not even asking for a detailed enumeration of the obligations and duties that this involved.

When Israel voiced its eagerness to receive the Torah, God spoke to Moses again: "Go unto the people, and sanctify them today and tomorrow, and let them wash their garments, and be ready against the third day; for on the third day the Lord will come down in the sight of all the people upon Mount Sinai. And thou shalt set bounds unto the people round about saying: Take heed to yourselves, that ye go not up onto the Mount, or touch the border of it, whosoever toucheth the Mount shall surely die."

Amid thunder and lightening the dawn of the third day broke. Heavy clouds hung over the mountains and growing sounds of the *shofar* made the children of Israel shake with fear. Moses led them out of the camp and placed them at the foot of Mount Sinai, which was completely covered by smoke and was quaking, for God had descended upon it in fire. The sound of the *shofar* grew louder. Suddenly, all sounds ceased. Then God proclaimed the Ten Commandments:

1. I am the Lord thy God, Who brought thee out of the land of Egypt, out of the house of bondage.
2. Thou shalt have no other gods before Me. Thou shalt not make unto thee a graven image, nor any manner of likeness, of any thing that is in heaven above, or that is in the earth beneath, or that is in the water under the earth; thou shalt not bow down unto them, nor serve them, for I, the Lord thy God, am a jealous God, visiting the iniquity of the fathers upon the children of the third and fourth generation of them that hate Me; and showing mercy unto the thousandth generation of them that love Me and keep My commandments.
3. Thou shalt not take the name of the Lord thy God in vain; for the Lord will not hold him guiltless that taketh His name in vain.

4. Remember the Sabbath day, to keep it holy. Six days shalt thou labor, and do all thy work; but the seventh day is a Sabbath unto the Lord thy God, in it thou shalt not do any manner of work, thou, nor thy servant, nor thy cattle, nor the stranger that is within thy gates; for in six days the Lord made heaven and earth, the sea and all that is in them, and rested on the seventh day, wherefore the Lord blessed the Sabbath day, and hallowed it.

5. Honor thy father and thy mother, that thy days may be long upon the land which the Lord thy God giveth thee.

6. Thou shalt not murder.

7. Thou shalt not commit adultery.

8. Thou shalt not steal.

9. Thou shalt not bear false witness against thy neighbor.

10. Thou shalt not covet thy neighbor's house; thou shalt not covet thy neighbor's wife, nor his man-servant, nor his maid-servant, nor his ox, nor his ass, nor anything that is thy neighbor's.

People trembled when they heard the words of God. They begged Moses to serve as their intermediary; if God Himself continued to give them the entire Torah, they feared they would surely die. Moses told them not to be afraid, for God had revealed Himself to them so that they would listen to Him and not sin.

Moses, the only man able to stand in the presence of God, then ascended the mountain. He remained there for forty days and forty nights, with neither food nor sleep; he had become like an angel. During this time, Moses received the two tablets containing the Ten Commandments and the entire Torah, which he was to teach to the children of Israel.

As you read the Commandments you saw that God calls himself a jealous God. Many years ago, this thought captured the imagination of a philosopher who turned for advice to one of his friends, a rabbi.

"Your God, in his Book, calls himself a jealous God who can endure no other god besides himself, and on all occasions makes known his abhorrence of idolatry. Why, then, does He threaten and seem to hate the worshippers of false gods more than the false gods themselves?"

Peering over his glasses, the rabbi replied: "A certain king had a disobedient son. Among other worthless tricks of various kinds, he had the baseness to give his father's name and titles to his dogs. To whom should the king show his anger, the prince or the dogs?"

"Well said," rejoined the philosopher, "but if your God destroyed the objects of idolatry, He would take away the temptation to worship them."

"Yes, if the fools only worshipped things that were of no use. But they worship the sun, the moon, the hosts of heaven; the rivers, the sea; fire, air, and what not. Would you have the Creator, for the sake of these fools, ruin His own works and disturb the laws appointed to nature by His own wisdom? If a man steals grain and sows it, should the seed not shoot up out of the earth because it was stolen? Oh, no! The wise Creator lets nature run her own course, for her course is His own appointment. And what if the children of folly abuse it to evil? The day of reckoning is not far off."

Now that you have reached the age of religious maturity, you must guard against becoming one of "the children of folly." God has endowed you with certain potentialities, but he has left to you the task of molding this raw material into the type of person you desire to be.

As you fashion your future, give serious thought to your proper relationship to God. Familiarize yourself with some of the important writings about God, so that you may gain an appreciation of how the bond between the Jewish people and the Almighty has enabled our religion to endure and to grow

58

to meet the needs of each new generation. Above all, let the message that we find in Psalms be your guide through life:

"The Lord is nigh unto all them that call upon Him."

chapter 5

SERVICE OF THE HEART

On the Day of Atonement, an orphaned boy, unable to read, brought with him to the Synagogue a large, heavy prayer book. He laid it on the reader's table and cried out tearfully: "Lord of Creation! I do not know how to pray, so here I give Thee the entire prayer book."

The Lord noted his sincerity and heard his plea. He was moved by the child's prayer.

SERVICE OF THE HEART

A young boy, age 10, was reciting his daily prayers. His mother, passing by, listened in.

"Dear God," she heard him say, "please give daddy a raise so that I can get my new bicycle. And please see that mother buys me a complete camping outfit, and a transistor radio."

At this point his mother interrupted him: "Never mind issuing orders," she said, "you just report for duty."

Like the young boy, many of us think of prayer in terms of requesting certain benefits; asking for specific personal favors. But is this prayer? Or is prayer rather reporting to hear what God wants us to do?

When we turn to God in prayer we are obeying an instinct planted in the soul by the Creator Himself. We are following a pattern of behavior that cuts across time and nations: the American Indian sprinkling corn meal in front of his tepee; the Chinese coolie bowing before the shrine of his ancestors; the Tibetan monk working his prayer wheel; the Jew sitting in awed reverence in his synagogue. Each expresses, in his own way, the universal conviction that we are not alone, that we depend for our good upon an outside power greater than man.

The Talmud calls prayer, *tefillah*, "the divine service of the heart." Through the ages people have used prayer to tell God their woe, make confession of sin, and ask for pardon and help.

64

Prayer, moreover, isn't something you do and then stop doing. It cannot be regarded as an umbrella to be used only when it is raining. If you pray sincerely, you carry your prayers wherever you go.

Prayer is based upon the idea of a covenant between God and man. It is an individual's reaction to the sorrows and joys of daily life. It ranges from a petition for help in distress to the highest form of thanks; from confession of sin to joyful expression of association with God. It is our attachment to the Almighty, the hymn book of all humanity. To pray is to build a spiritual ladder to our Creator. It takes a person out of the narrowness of self-interest; it is an effective method overcoming our human weaknesses. Prayer teaches us what to aspire to and gives us an ideal to cherish.

To pray is to recognize the wonder of creation. It is a person's humble answer to the mystery of life. It is an invitation to God to intervene in one's life, to let His will prevail in one's affairs. It is the opening of a window to Him. It is an effort to make Him the Lord of our soul. Through praying man conquers his fears.

Henry Ward Beecher, who devoted his life to human decency, described prayer in these words: "Prayer covers the whole of a man's life. There is no thought, feeling, yearning or desire, however low, trifling or vulgar we may deem it, which, if it affects our real interest or happiness, we may not lay before God to be sure of sympathy. His nature is such that our often coming does not tire Him. The whole burden, of the whole life, of every man may be rolled on to God and not weary Him, though it has wearied the man."

One day, shortly after Israel had successfully finished fighting a war to defend her borders, a veteran who had lost a leg in battle, appeared at the home of a rabbi to receive a blessing. As he hobbled along in obvious pain, someone remarked: "That poor silly man, does he think that the rabbi can ask God to give him back his leg?"

The young veteran overheard the remark and, turning slowly on his one good leg, said: "Of course I do not expect

God to give me back my leg. I merely come to pray to God to help me live without it."

We must understand that God has given us prayer not to obtain the good things of earth, but to learn to do without them; not to help escape evil, but to make us strong enough to meet it. We cannot conceive of God as a bell-hop for whom we need only press a buzzer to get things done. The wise know that prayer is rather the opening of the heart and mind to hear the voice of God. Prayer acts something like the one-way telephones used by automobiles and airplanes. From the air you can talk to the ground and from the ground you can talk to the air, but you can't do both at the same time.

An important element in any prayer is not what we say to God, but what God says to us. It is like turning on an electric switch. Flicking the switch does not create the current, it simply provides a channel through which the electric current may flow. Some of us are so harried in the course of our daily lives that we are apt to pray and then hurry away without giving God a chance to answer. We must remember that prayer is more than speaking to God; it is giving God an opportunity to speak to us.

Of course, prayer must never be a substitute for effort. A rabbi once taught this in an object lesson to a young man who had expressed doubt about the validity of the motto, "Pray and Work." He invited him to go rowing but took only one oar into the boat with him. The young man, who by now was perplexed at the rabbi's strange actions, commented, "Rabbi, if you use only one oar, you will continue to go round in circles and you won't go anywhere."

"Just what I am trying to prove!" replied the rabbi. "One oar is called prayer and the other is called work. Unless you use both at the same time, you just travel in circles and don't get anywhere."

Rabbi Abraham J. Feldman wrote: "There was a little girl who was on her way to school and she was afraid of being late. She turned to her sister and said, "Let us stop running and pray that we may not be late." She missed the point in prayer. Her sister was wiser, for she replied, "Let's pray while we run."

66

Similarly, a wise man once advised: "Pray as if everything depends on God, and work as if everything depends on you." In other words, pray as though no work would help, and work as though no prayer would help. Don't make the mistake of the boy who, to his surprise and dismay, failed his final examinations.

"How much studying did you do for the examinations?" asked his teacher.

"I didn't study at all," he answered, "I thought that if you asked God to help you, that was all you had to do."

During World War II, a chaplain emphasized the idea of prayer and action in the heat of a naval battle when he comforted the men on his ship with the words, "Praise the Lord and pass the ammunition."

And on the night of July 10, 1943, General Dwight D. Eisenhower, who was to become President of the United States, demonstrated his appreciation of this principle while he watched a vast armada of 3,000 ships sail across from Malta to the shores of Sicily for a great battle. The general saluted his heroic men and then bowed his head in prayer. To an officer beside him, Eisenhower explained: "There comes a time when you've used your brains, your training, your technical skill, and the die is cast and the events are in the hands of God, and there you have to leave them."

While prayer is a source of strength and in many instances has a greater power than medicine or science, it must mean something to you if it is to mean anything to God. The Ba'al Shem Tov, the father of Chasidism, wrote many many years ago: "Let your prayer be a window to Heaven." Prayer is conversation with God. In the words of Eliezer ben Hycranus: "When you pray, know before whom you stand."

It is not the arithmetic of your prayers, how many they are; nor the rhetoric of your prayers, how eloquent they are; nor the geometry of your prayers, how long they are; nor the music of your prayers, how melodious they are; nor the logic of your prayers, how carefully argued they are; nor even the theology of your prayers, how good the doctrine—which God cares for. Sincerity, *kavanah*, fervency of spirit is what He looks for.

Prayer cannot be thought of as some magical formula that grants man his desires. Too often prayer sounds more like advice than supplication. Remember, there is a difference between "to pray" and "to pray *for*." Prayer requires equal portions of faith and patience. Pray with confidence, because if you pray without confidence you cannot hope to have your prayers answered.

Numerous illustrations of individual prayers are found in our holy writings. King David, his body agonized and his mind troubled by ill wishers who taunted him, cried out to God:

> O, Lord rebuke me not in Thine anger
> Neither chasten me in Thy wrath.
> Be gracious unto me, O Lord, for I languish away;
> Heal me, O Lord, for my bones are affrighted ...

In Exodus, when Moses and the Jews successfully crossed the Red Sea, we read:

> Then sang Moses and the children of Israel this song
>   unto the Lord, and spoke, saying:
> I will sing unto the Lord, for He is highly exalted;
> The horse and his rider has He thrown into the sea.
> The Lord is my strength and song,
> And He is become my salvation;
> This is my God, and I will glorify Him;
> My father's God, and I will exalt Him.

Many of the prayers which have become part of the synagogue service were written by the Sages of the Talmud. Among the most meaningful and inspiring are these:

Prayer for the coming month: "May it be Thy will, O Lord our God and God of our fathers, to renew unto us this coming month for good and for blessing. To grant us long life, a life of peace, a life of good, a life of blessing, a life of sustenance, a life of bodily vigor, a life marked by the fear of Heaven and the dread of sin, a life free from shame and reproach, a life of prosperity and honor, a life in which the love of Torah and the fear of

68

Heaven shall cleave to us, a life wherein Thou fulfillest all the desires of our heart for good."

Prayer following the Amidah: "O my God! Guard my tongue from evil and my lips from speaking guile; and to such as curse me let my soul be dumb, yea, let my soul be unto all as the dust. Open my heart to Thy Torah, and let my soul pursue Thy Commandments. . . ."

Prayer to be offered in time of danger: "Do Thy will in heaven above; grant tranquillity of spirit to those who fear Thee below, and do that which is good in Thy sight. Blessed art Thou, O Lord, Who hearkenest unto prayer."

Prayer to be said on waking in the morning: "Blessed art Thou, O Lord, Who revivest the dead. My Lord, I have sinned before Thee. May it be acceptable before Thee, O Lord my God, that Thou grant me a good heart, a happy lot, a good inclination, a good friend, a good name, a generous eye, a liberal soul and a humble spirit. . . ."

One who is about to pray can learn from the laborer who sometimes takes a whole day to prepare for a job. The woodcutter, who spends most of the day sharpening his saw and only the last hour cutting the wood, has earned the day's wage. Do not let your prayers become perfunctory. When you have two minutes of prayer, spend one of them in preparation. A rabbi was asked: "What do you do before you pray?" With deep sincerity he replied: "I pray that when I pray, I may pray with all my heart." The prophet Isaiah warned against those who hypocritically appeal to God with prayers that are not sincere.

Once the Baal Shem Tov stopped on the threshold of a house of prayer and refused to enter. "I cannot go in," he said, "the synagogue is crowded with prayers from wall to wall and from floor to ceiling. How could there be room for me?"

When he saw that those around were staring at him, he explained: "The words from the lips of those who pray, which do not come from the heart, cannot rise unto heaven. They remain to fill the house from wall to wall and from floor to ceiling."

He who prays without knowing what he prays, does not pray. In the *Sefer Ha-hasidim*, it is said, "Let those who do not know Hebrew learn the prayers in their own vernacular, for prayer must be understood. If the heart does not know what the lips utter, it is no prayer."

In Hasidic literature we read of the ignorant peasant who entered the synagogue. For a minute or two he listened to the scholars intone their beautiful prayers. Since he, too, wished to express his love of God, he faced the Holy Ark and began repeating the letters of the Hebrew alphabet over and over again.

Here and there people nudged each other, commenting on the man's obvious ignorance. Suddenly, a silence descended upon the entire synagogue as they heard him say: "Lord of the universe, I am a simple, ignorant man. I yearn to have the words to fashion beautiful prayers to praise Thee! But, alas, I cannot find them. Please God, listen as I recite the letters of the alphabet. You, who know how I feel and what is in my heart, fashion these letters into words, and the words into sentences that express my great love for You." And after a moment or two of silence, he resumed his prayers: "Alef, Bet, Gimel...."

Jewish prayer started with Abraham. Later, after the destruction of the Temple, the Sages adopted the method of communing with God by offering prayers at certain fixed times, seasons and occasions. Prayers were fixed for three times a day and were to be recited in a set order. Our Talmudists say that Abraham instituted the *Shacharit* (morning prayer), Isaac the *Mincha* (afternoon prayer) and Jacob the *Maariv* (evening prayer).

The habit of prayer is part of our religious life. In addition to praying in the morning, afternoon and evenings we pray on all important occasions. At times we offer individual, private prayers. For example, when boys and girls take important examinations they frequently pray to God for guidance, or having passed these examinations, they offer thanks to the Almighty.

70

At home and in the synagogue we pray from a *Siddur* (prayer book). Some people have questioned the use of the Siddur. "Why," they ask, "must we have this formalized set of printed prayers? Why can't we pray in any way we wish?" The truth is that in a synagogue, if everyone wanted to pray in his own way, confusion might be the end result. We can be sincere even if we use the same prayer as our neighbor. After all, we all use the same words when we pledge allegiance to our flag. Consideration must also be given to those who just can't find the right words to use in praying.

The Siddur is one of the most important books in Jewish life because it embodies the joys and sorrows, the hopes and aspirations of many generations. Interwoven in the prayers are passages from the Bible, the Mishna, the Talmud and the Zohar, as well as from the poetic philosophic creations of our people. It includes half of the book of Psalms, all of the Song of Songs, and many excerpts from the Five Books of Moses and the Prophets. The Siddur has rightfully been termed the mother tongue that binds Israel.

The Siddur is not the work of one man or one age. It has grown with the centuries and has undergone changes which reflect the dispersal of the Jews among the nations of the world. At first, all Jews used the same Siddur. But it was only natural for them to make changes in it that suited their particular needs and environments. This explains the differences we find between the *Sephardic* prayer book used in Spain and the *Ashkenazic* one used in Poland. Sometimes the difference is merely in the order of prayers, sometimes the difference is in the prayers themselves. Yet, despite the changes made, the most important features of worship are contained in every type of Siddur.

Rabbi Joseph H. Hertz, who during his life served as Chief Rabbi of Great Britain, wrote about the development of Sephardic and Ashkenazic prayers in the introduction to his Daily Prayer Book. He states that the Ashkenazic rite is now dominant in English speaking lands.

To many the Siddur is a daily companion; every word of it is familiar and loved. No other volume has penetrated the

71

Jewish home as has the Siddur. Millions of Jews go to its pages for weekday and Sabbath services.

The *Machzor* (Festival Prayer Book) as contrasted to the Siddur is designed especially for use during holidays. There is a Machzor for the *Yomim Noraim* (Days of Awe) as well as for the *Sholosh Regolim* (Three Major Festivals): *Pesach, Shevuot* and *Sukkot.* The word Machzor comes from the Hebrew root *chazer,* which means "cycle" or "to repeat."

The synagogue service has been called an expression of the soul of collective Israel. The congregants are led in prayer by the *shaliach tzibbur,* or *chazzan,* who is the representative of the congregation before God through the medium of prayers. He is not an intermediary; merely a messenger of the congregation.

The principal prayer has always been the *Shema:* "Hear, O Israel, The Lord our God, the Lord is One!" It is called the *Shema* because "Shema" is the first word of the verse in Hebrew. As we saw in Chapter IV, the *Shema* has always been the watchword, the motto, the foundation of the Jewish faith. It is usually the first prayer that the Jewish child learns to recite. It is the last prayer the dying Jew repeats before he yields his soul to God. Throughout our history, the *Shema* has been recited by the Jew in every crisis; it is the Jewish affirmation of faith in God.

King Solomon said: "In the multitude of people is the King's glory." This indicates that it is the duty of each Jew to make an effort to pray with a *minyan,* a quorum, consisting of ten male adults. It is felt that congregational prayer not only creates greater religious sentiment and enthusiasm than individual prayer but that it also has the advantage of uniting many hearts in prayer to our common Father. Interestingly, these congregational prayers are generally said in the plural and call for the coming of the Messiah and the restoration of Israel. Jews everywhere pray for universal peace and the brotherhood of man.

Aime Palliere, a French Catholic studying for the priesthood, who once entered a synagogue on Yom Kippur at the time of the *Neilah Amidah* (silent devotion), described his reaction to the first Jewish service he attended as follows:

"That which revealed itself to me at that moment was not the Jewish faith. It was the Jewish people. The spectacle of that large number of Jewish men assembled, their shoulders covered by the *talit*, suddenly disclosed to my eyes a far-off past. The Hebrews of the Bible were there on their feet before me. Two details struck me particularly about the faithful bent over their ritual. At first, on seeing the prayer shawls worn uniformly by all the participants in the service, I thought that in a way they were all officiating. In the second place, it seemed to me that this silent assembly was expecting something to happen. 'What are they waiting for?' I asked my companion. Here were revealed to me two characteristics of this misunderstood people and its great faith: the form of collective priesthood which characterizes Judaism, and the spirit of expectancy and of faith in the future which stamps its entire cult with a special zeal."

Perhaps one final reason for prayer can be found in a story related by the Sages and handed down by memory from generation to generation. When God finished the world, the Sages said, He asked one of the angels if anything was still lacking on land or on sea, in the air or in heaven. The angel answered that all was perfect, but one thing was still desired, *speech* to praise God's work.

Ruth F. Brin in her volume of poems and prayers for our day entitled, "A Time To Search," captured the mood in a poem entitled "Worship." She writes:

"Among the many appetites of man
    There is a craving after God.

Among the many attributes of man
    There is a talent for worshipping God.

Jews who wandered in deserts beneath the stars
    Knew their hearts were hungry for God.

73

Jews who studied in candle-lit ghetto rooms
Thirsted longingly after God.

But we who are smothered with comfort
Sometimes forget to listen for God.

Help us, O Lord, to recognize our need,
To hear the yearning whisper of our hearts.

Help us to seek the silence of the desert
And the thoughtfulness of the house of study.

Bless us, like our fathers in ancient days,
With that most precious gift: a sense of Thy presence.

Brush us with the wind of the wings of Thy Being,
Fill us with the awe of Thy holiness.
We, too, will praise, glorify and exalt Thy name."

We pray to thank God, for all that He has given us. And
we pray also to achieve a sense of closeness to God, to feel His
presence. The Holy Father is not far away. He is as near as
the mouth is to the ear. Pray and He will answer.

74

chapter 6

THE GOOD LIFE

When man appears before the throne of judgment, the first question he will be asked is not, "Have you believed in God?" or "Have you prayed?" or "Have you performed the rituals properly?" He will be asked, "Have you been honorable and faithful in all your dealings with your fellow man?"

The Talmud

"And they shall beat their swords
into plowshares,
And their spears into pruning
hooks;
Nation shall not lift up sword
against nation,
Neither shall they learn war
anymore."

ISAIAH

THE GOOD LIFE

There is, of course, no short-cut to maturity. In the eyes of society, at thirteen you are still a young man or young woman who has some way to go before reaching adulthood. At times you will no doubt find this condition most irritating, but it is best that you recognize its value as a period of preparation for life and take full advantage of it. For, as we are taught in Proverbs, "He that is patient is governed with much wisdom; but he that is impatient, exalteth his folly."

Nevertheless, you are considered sufficiently mature by your people to assume an attitude, a posture, a way of life that is based upon the loftiest ideals of its teachings about man's relationship to his fellow man. And it should be stressed that from the biblical command, "These are the judgments which thou shalt set before them," it is clear that this applies to the Bar Mitzvah as well as to the girl who has reached religious maturity.

Some time ago, a rabbi and a soap manufacturer went for a walk together. As they walked along the city streets, the manufacturer turned to the rabbi and asked: "Rabbi, of what value is religion? After thousands of years of teaching about goodness, truth, honesty, respect . . . after all the prayers offered and sermons preached there still is so much trouble and misery in the world. If religion is beneficial, why should this be?"

78

The rabbi continued walking as he mulled the question over in his mind. Soon they reached a crowded street filled with boys and girls playing in the gutter. Many of them were filthy with sweat and grime. The rabbi, pointing to one particularly dirty child said, "Look at that child. He is about the dirtiest youngster I've ever seen. You say that soap makes people clean but you can almost peel the dirt off that boy. What good is soap? We have so much soap in the world and this child is still filthy! I question the effectiveness of soap."

The manufacturer, protesting, stopped in his tracks and said: "That's not fair rabbi, soap can't do any good until it is used!"

"This is just the point," replied the rabbi. "So it is with religion. It too is not effective unless it is used!"

It is this failure to use religion, to truly live by its principles, that makes a mockery of religion. We cannot say we believe in the Ten Commandments and at the same time fail to abide by them. Belief and moral action are indivisible. To believe without demonstrating our belief through our deeds is an admission of moral weakness.

Indeed, as Morris Joseph once wrote, "Judaism is something more than a badge, something more than a birth-mark; it is a life. To be born a Jew does not declare any of us to be of the elect; it only designates us for enrollment among the elect. God signs the covenant, but we have to seal it—to seal it by a life of service. Two things make a man a Jew: membership in the Jewish brotherhood, and loyal fulfillment of the obligations which that membership imposes. To be of the Jewish race but to trample upon Jewish duty is to be faithless to Israel."

What are the responsibilities of the thirteen year old Jew? In previous chapters, we discussed *tefillin*, prayer, belief in God, and the need for attending religious services. There are additional moral requisites that the mature Jew must observe, for example, respect for parents, honesty, justice, equality, truth, assistance to the oppressed. The Jew must always consider himself part of the community; as was taught thousands of years ago, he *is* "his brother's keeper."

The Talmud asks, "What is the right course that a man should choose for himself?" And it answers: "That which he feels to be honorable to himself, and which also brings him honor from mankind. Who is honored? He who honors others." Our Sages have also said, "There are three crowns: the crown of Torah, the crown of priesthood and the crown of royalty, but the crown of a good name excels them all."

So, speak not evil of anyone; seek the love and respect of your neighbor. All of us can give friendship to those who yearn for it; loyalty to those who depend upon us; courtesy to those with whom we come in contact; kindness to those whose paths we may cross; understanding to those whose views may not be in accord with our own. If you make the next person feel he is worthwhile, he will see you in the same light. The prayer of each of us might well be: "Lord, give me the courage to change what can be changed; the patience to bear what cannot be changed; the wisdom to tell one from the other."

A lesson in concern for others was given by a woman who was the object of much curiosity in her neighborhood because of a most unusual habit. Every time she shopped, went to eat in a restaurant, or went to see a motion picture, she would take a little book out of her purse and write in it.

"Do you keep a record of all your expenditures?" someone finally asked her.

"Not at all," she replied. "I only keep a list of what I spend for luxuries."

"What for?" asked the slightly bewildered questioner.

"I feel," answered the woman, "that if I am able to enjoy the comforts of life in the midst of so much poverty in the world, I should donate part of my luxury to the homeless and the sick."

As man developed he realized more and more the necessity of helping his fellow man in times of stress. When a Jew makes a contribution, he is considered to be giving *zedakah* (dispensing justice) by returning to society a portion of what he has received from it. However, the Jew is taught not to look for praise for every good deed he does. "He who gives charity in secret is greater than Moses," say our ancient scholars.

80

Maimonides set up what is called "the Golden Ladder of Charity." He wrote:

There are eight degrees of charity-giving.

The first and lowest degree is to give—but with reluctance or regret. This is the gift of the hand, but not of the heart.

The second is to give cheerfully—but not in proportion to the distress of the sufferer.

The third is to give cheerfully and proportionately—but not until we are solicited.

The fourth is to give cheerfully, proportionately and even unsolicited—but to put it in the poor man's hand, thereby arousing in him the painful emotion of shame.

The fifth is to give charity in such a way that the distressed may receive the bounty and know their benefactor, without their being known to him. Such was the conduct of some of our ancestors, who used to tie up money in the hind-corners of of their cloaks, so that the poor might take it unperceived.

The sixth, which rises still higher, is to know the objects of our bounty, but remain unknown to them. Such was the conduct of those of our ancestors who used to convey their charitable gifts into poor people's dwellings, taking care that their own persons and names should remain unknown.

The seventh, still more meritorious, is to bestow charity in such a way that the benefactor may not know the recipient, nor he, the name of his benefactor, as was done by our charitable forefathers during the existence of the Temple. For there was in that holy building a place called the "Chamber of Silence," wherein the good deposited

81

secretly whatever generous hearts suggested, and from which the most respectable poor families were maintained with equal secrecy.

The eighth, and the most meritorious of all, is to anticipate charity by preventing poverty; namely, to assist the reduced brother, either by a considerable gift, or a loan of money, or by teaching him a trade, or by setting him up in business, so that he may earn an honest livelihood and not be forced to the dreadful alternative of holding up his hand for charity. And to this Scripture alludes when it says, "And if thy brother be waxen poor, and fallen in disrepute with thee, then thou shalt relieve him; yea, though he be a stranger or a sojourner, that he may live with thee." This is the highest step and the summit of charity's "Golden Ladder."

As far back as the year 1300, Asher ben Yechiel wrote what may today be considered a guide for human relations:

"Be not ready to quarrel; avoid oaths and passionate adjurations, excess of laughter and outbursts of wrath; they disturb and confound the reason of man. Avoid all dealings where there is a lie. Utter not the name of God superfluously, or in dirty places.

"Cut from under you all mere human supports, and make not gold the foremost longing of your life; for that is the first step to idolatry. Rather give money than words; and as to ill words, see that you place them in the scale of understanding before they leave your lips.

"What has been uttered in your presence, even though not told as secret, let it not pass from you to others. And if one tell you a tale, say not to him that you heard it before. Do not fix your eyes too much on one who is far above you in worldly fortune.

"Put no one to shame; misuse not your power against anyone; who can tell whether you will not some day be powerless yourself.

"Do not struggle for the small triumph of showing yourself in the right and a wise man in the wrong; you are not one bit the wiser therefore. Be not angry or unkind to anyone for trifles, lest you make yourself enemies unnecessarily.

"Do not refuse things out of mere obstinacy to your fellow-citizens; rather put your will below their wishes. Avoid, as much as may be possible, bad men, men of persistent angry feelings, fools; you can get nothing from their company but shame. Be the first to extend courteous greeting to every man, whatever be his faith; provoke not to wrath one of another belief not your own."

Another valuable lesson in human relations can be learned from the following story:

High up in the Rockies there lived a small boy and his mother. One day, after he had been punished severely, the lad ran to the edge of a precipice and shouted back at his mother, "I hate you! I hate you!" Across the ravine came the echo: "I hate you! I hate you!"

Frightened, the boy ran back to his mother and sobbed: "Who is the bad man over there who shouted, 'I hate you!'"

Taking the boy's hand, the mother led him back to the edge of the precipice. "Now son," she said, "Call out, I love you! I love you!" The boy did as he was told. Clearly and sweetly the echo came: "I love you! I love you!"

"My child," said the mother, "that is the law of life. What you give, you get." King Solomon advised: "Cast thy bread upon the running waters and in the fullness of time it will return to you."

"There are four characters among men," we are taught in *The Ethics of the Fathers*. "He who says, 'What is mine is mine and what is yours is yours,' he is a neutral character; some say, this is a character like that of the people of Sodom. He who says, 'What is yours is mine and what is mine is yours,' he is a boor. He who says, 'What is mine is yours and what is yours is yours,' he is a saint. He who says, 'What is yours is mine and what is mine is mine,' he is a wicked man."

The right type of boys and girls will try to live a good life for its own sake, and not for some material reward. An old Jewish teacher once said: "Be not like servants who serve their master in order to receive a reward, but like servants who serve their master without expectation of reward."

Abraham, Moses, Isaiah, Hillel . . . they all sought to make their life good and pure without expecting any special compensation. Moses followed the Divine command to free Israel from bondage. He devoted himself to this task not for the sake of material reward; he simply wanted to do what was right. It was this same feeling that prompted Abraham, Isaiah, Hillel and the host of other holy men to do right for its own sake.

Of course, a good life brings its own rewards, just as an evil life brings penalties. A good life is richer because it contains more worth. You will certainly agree that the rich man is the one who has the most wisdom, not the largest balance sheet. We find a beautiful illustration of this in one of the dreams of King Solomon.

Solomon was still young at the time. He loved the Lord and tried to follow in the footsteps of his father. When the Lord, in a dream, offered to give him whatever he asked, Solomon prayed for an understanding heart, that he might discern between good and evil. He did not ask for riches, nor for power, nor for a long life, but for wisdom; the sort of wisdom that would lead to goodness. It is true that Solomon became a very rich and mighty king. But his wisdom was his real wealth. It put more beauty and riches into his life than could come from any other form of wealth. When Solomon forgot the wisdom of goodness, which he had loved so dearly as a young man, all his other riches were of little use.

Man is the most marvelous creature on earth, the pride of creation. God has blessed him with the supreme gift of reason and endowed him with mind and soul. The Psalmist states: "The heavens are the heavens of the Lord, but the earth hath He given to the children of men." Thus, man is made the ruler of this vast and beautiful world, and he becomes responsible for what happens to it.

Maimonides summarizes the philosophy that should be the basis of the every-day life of the Jew in what has been called, "A Father's Admonition:"

Fear the Lord the God of your Fathers and serve Him in love, for fear only restrains a man from sin, while love stimulates him to good. Accustom yourself to habitual goodness, for a man's character is what habit makes it. The perfection of the body is a necessary antecedent to the perfection of the soul, for health is the key to the inner chamber. If you find in the Law or the Prophets or the Sages a profound saying which you cannot understand, stand fast by your faith and attribute the fault to your want of intelligence. Place it in a corner of your heart for future consideration, but despise not your religion because you are unable to understand one difficult matter.

Love truth and uprightness, the ornaments of the soul, and cleave unto them; prosperity so obtained is built on a sure rock. Keep firmly to your word; let not a legal contract or witnesses be more binding than your verbal promise whether in public or in private. Disdain reservations and subterfuges, evasions and sharp practices. Woe to him who builds his house upon them. Abhor inactivity and indolence, the causes of destruction of body, of penury, of self contempt, the ladders of Satan and his satellites.

Defile not your soul by quarrelsomeness and petulance. I have seen the white become black, the low brought still lower, families driven into exile, princes deposed from their high estate, great cities laid in ruins, assemblies dispersed, the pious humiliated, the honorable held lightly and despised, all on account of quarrelsomeness. Glory in forbearance, for in that is true strength and victory.

chapter 7

TEACHERS OF OUR RELIGION

"As a little wood can set light to a great tree, so young pupils sharpen the wits of great scholars. Rabbi Chanina said: 'Much Torah have I learned from my teachers, more from my colleagues, but from my students most of all.'"

Talmud Ta'anit 7a

"One generation shall laud Thy
works to another,
And shall declare Thy
mighty acts."

PSALMS

TEACHERS OF
OUR RELIGION

Who were the first teachers of Judaism? What books did they use before the books we use today were published? How did they go about spreading the concepts of Judaism?

The Patriarchs, Abraham, Isaac and Jacob were the first teachers of our religion. In Chapter IV, you read how Abraham refused to believe in idols and how he defied King Nimrod. Abraham actually was the very first teacher of our religion. At God's command, *Lech Lecha* (Get thee out of thy country), he left his father's house in Chaldea to devote the rest of his life to the service of the Almighty. According to the Rabbis, God said to Abraham: "Many precepts hast thou fulfilled, many good deeds hast thou performed, yet thou hast become like them. Travel from place to place, and thy name will become great."

Genesis declares: "And Abram took Sarai his wife, and Lot his brother's son, and all their substance that they gathered, and the souls that they had made in Haran; and they went forth to go into the land of Canaan." Rabbi Elazar bar Zimra offered the following comment on this: "If all people in the world should attempt to create a single insect they would be unable to breathe the breath of life into it, and here it is said, 'And the souls *they* had made in Haran.' What the Scripture really refers to is the proselytes they won to their way of life. And why does Scripture use the term *made* for the winning of proselytes? It is to teach us that whoever draws a pagan close to himself and influences him to become a proselyte, it is as though he had begotten him." Thus, Abraham became the father of the Jewish nation which included many proselytes. Tradition states that Abraham converted the men to the true worship of God as Sarah spread the Divine law among the women.

A disciple once asked his rabbi: "In the Talmud we read that Abraham kept all the laws. How could this be, since they had not yet been given to him?"

"All that is needed," the teacher replied, "is to love God. If you are about to do something and you think it might lessen your love, then you will know it is sin. If you are about to do something and think it will increase your love, you will know that your will is in keeping with the will of God. This is what Abraham did."

It was Abraham's custom to sit at his tent door waiting to entertain strangers. One day he saw an old man, weary with age and travel, coming toward him. Abraham received him kindly, washed his feet and provided him with supper. When Abraham observed that the old man ate without a prayer, he asked him why he did not worship the God in heaven. The old man told him that he worshipped fire only, and acknowledged no other God. When Abraham heard this he became angry and forced the old man out of his tent into the night.

After the old man had departed, God called to Abraham and asked where the stranger was. Abraham replied: "I asked him to leave because he did not worship Thee."

God remonstrated: "I have suffered with him for eighty years although he dishonored Me, and you could not endure him for one night?" Then Abraham rushed out into the night, overtook the stranger and brought him back into his tent, where he accorded him hospitality and wise instruction.

The Prophets followed the Patriarchs as teachers of God. Their chief aim in life was to teach the will of God. Again and again these far-visioned, pious men pleaded with the people to lead righteous lives.

Moses was the greatest of our Prophets. In Deuteronomy we read: "A prophet has never arisen in Israel like unto Moses." He

was the deliverer, law-giver and teacher of Israel. He gave us the Decalogue—the Ten Commandments. In the name of God he said: "If you will hearken unto My voice, indeed, and keep My covenant, then ye shall be Mine own treasure among all peoples; and ye shall be unto Me a kingdom of priests and a holy nation."

Moses was tested by God through sheep. The Rabbis tell us that while Moses was attending Jethro's flock in the wilderness, a lamb strayed from the herd. Moses endeavored to overtake it, but it ran much faster than he could run. Then it came upon a fountain, and suddenly it stopped and took a drink of water.

"You dear little innocent creature," said Moses, "I see now why you ran away. Had I known your want, on my shoulders would I have carried you to the fountain to quench your thirst. But come little innocent one, I will make up for my ignorance. You are no doubt fatigued after so long a journey; you shall walk no further." He immediately took the little creature into his arms, and carried it back to the flock.

God approved of the deed, and a heavenly voice was heard to exclaim. "Moses, benevolent Moses! If a dumb animal thus excited your compassion, how much more will the children of men! What will you not do for your own brethren? Come, from now on you shall be the shepherd of my chosen flock, and you will teach them by your example 'that the Lord is good to all, and that His mercies are over all His works.'"

There are many other stories about Moses. Rabbi Joshua ben Levi said: "When Moses heard about the suffering of the children of Israel, he exclaimed before God: 'Master of the universe, let Moses and a hundred like him perish rather than the fingernail of even one Israelite be injured.'"

After Moses received the precepts from God, he taught them to Aaron; then, in Aaron's presence, to Aaron's sons; then, in the presence of Aaron and his sons, to the seventy elders of Israel; finally, in the presence of all these disciples, to the whole people of Israel. After Moses' departure, the entire procedure was repeated with Aaron serving as the teacher. After Aaron finished, his sons served as teachers, repeating the precepts to the people for the fourth time. It would seem that each party studied the

Torah four times outright. Thus, it was fully and permanently retained in the memory of both the leaders and the people.

After forty years in the desert, and five weeks before his death, Moses repeated the Torah to the children of Israel for the last time, and again explained it to them thoroughly. Tradition tells us that the Torah also was written down in thirteen copies, one for each of the twelve tribes and one for the Holy Ark in the Sanctuary.

Over and over the Prophets proclaimed that an unrighteous life was not worth living. The Prophet Isaiah warned against those who hypocritically appeal to God with prayers, but are obviously immoral and dishonest in their actions:

> And when ye spread forth your hands,
> I will hide Mine eyes from you;
> Yea, when ye make many prayers,
> I will not hear;
> Your hands are full of blood.
> Wash you, make you clean,
> Put away the evil of your doings
> From before Mine eyes,
> Cease to do evil;
> Learn to do well;
> Seek justice, relieve the oppressed,
> Judge the fatherless, plead for the widow.

And then, in an attempt to counsel, he said:

> Seek the Lord while He may be found
> Call upon Him while He is near.

Another Prophet, Micah, taught:

> It hath been told thee, O man,
> What is good, and what the Lord doth require of thee.
> Only to do justly, and to love mercy
> And to walk humbly with thy God.

Amos preached;

> Take away from me the noise of your songs;
> I will not listen to the melody of your lyres.
> But let justice roll down like waters,
> And righteousness like a perennial stream . . .
> Perhaps then the Lord, the God of hosts,
> Will be gracious to a remnant of Joseph.

Jeremiah proclaimed:

> Thus says the Lord of hosts, the God of Israel to all the exiles whom I carried into exile from Jerusalem to Babylon: Build houses, and live in them; plant vineyards, and eat the fruit of them; take wives, and beget sons and daughters; take wives also for your sons, and give your daughters to husbands, that they may bear sons and daughters; so let your numbers increase, and not diminish. And seek the welfare of the land to which I have carried you into exile, and pray to the Lord on its behalf; for in its welfare shall you find your welfare.

In *Pirke Avot* ("The Ethics of the Fathers") we find many of the teachings of the great rabbis in Israel. In a sense, these rabbis were also prophets because their teachings applied to the world of tomorrow in which the children of today have to live. You can see this from the following:

> Rabbi Simeon, the son of Gamaliel said:
> By three things is the world preserved: by truth, by judgment and by peace. As it is said: "Judge ye the truth and the judgment of peace in your gates."

> Simon the Just taught:
> Upon three things the world is based: upon Torah, upon service, and upon the practice of charity.

Jose, the son of Joezer said:
Let thy house be a meeting house of the wise; sit amidst the dust of their feet, and drink their words with thirst.

Hillel said:
If I am not for myself, who will be for me? And if I am only for myself, what am I? And if not now, when?

Rabbi Eleazar ben Azariah said:
He whose wisdom exceeds his work, to what is he like? To a tree whose branches are many, but whose roots are few; and the wind comes and plucks it up and over-turns it upon its face.

Ben Zoma said:
Who is wise? He who can learn from every man. Who is strong? He who can control his passions. Who is rich? He who can feel satisfied with his lot. Who is honored? He who honors mankind.

Elisha ben Abuya said:
If one learns as a child, to what is it comparable? To writing on clean paper. And if one learns as an old man, to what is that comparable? To writing on blotted paper.

Rabbi Jochanan ben Zakkai once said to his disciples: "Go forth and find which is the greatest ethical quality that man should choose for his rule in life."
One suggested contentment.
Another thought friendship.
The third proposed neighborly love.
The fourth said weighing the consequences of one's actions.
The fifth contended that the greatest quality was a good heart.
The rabbi thereupon declared that he accepted the last opinion in preference to any other, "for in his idea all their ideas are included!"

95

From Moses on, every one of our leaders was a teacher as well. We are told that the tribe of Levi, in addition to their duties in the Temple, went from tribe to tribe and imparted religious instruction.

When the Prophets stopped prophesying the Sages became the teachers of religion. They, too, attempted to impress on the minds of the people the great moral lessons of the Prophets. We find examples of their teachings in the Mishna and Midrash.

In later years these teachers were known as Scribes, and still later on as Rabbis. When we think of Ezra and Jochanan ben Zakkai, we get a good idea of the Scribe and the Rabbi.

A writer once said, "Judaism and the Bible are by no means identical; the Bible is only one part of Judaism, though the most fundamental one. Who taught the average Jew to understand his Judaism, to love his religion and his God? Without the zeal of the Rabbis, the Bible would never have become the guide of every Jew. They translated it into the vernacular for the people and expounded it to the masses. They taught them not to despair under the tortures of the present, but to look forward to the future. At the same time, they developed the spirit of the Bible and never lost sight of the lofty teachings of the Prophets. It is the immortal merit of the unknown Rabbis of the centuries immediately before and after the common era that they found and applied the proper 'fences' for the preservation of Judaism, and that they succeeded in rescuing real morality and pure monotheism for the ages that were to follow."

In this group can be included the Chasidic rabbis who taught that God not only responds to the prayer of the leader, but that the humblest person in the congregation may bring the Divine Father into the lives of His children. There are many lessons that the Chasidic rabbis taught their disciples. The stories below show the simplicity with which they were able to convey great moral truths.

WIPING OUT EVIL

The disciples of a Chasidic rabbi approached their spiritual leader with a complaint about the prevalence of evil in the world.

Intent upon driving out the forces of darkness, they requested the rabbi to counsel them. The rabbi suggested that they take brooms and attempt to sweep the darkness from a cellar. The bewildered disciples applied themselves to sweeping out the darkness but to no avail.

The rabbi then advised this followers to take sticks and to beat vigorously at the darkness to drive out the evil. When this likewise failed, he counseled them to go down again into the cellar and to protest against the darkness and to shout imprecations to drive out the evil. When this, too, failed, he said: "My children, let each of you meet the challenge of darkness by lighting a candle." The disciples descended to the cellar and kindled their lights. They looked and behold, the darkness had been driven out. In this way the rabbi taught that it was incumbent upon man to drive out the darkness from the world by introducing light, which is the symbol of truth, goodness and wisdom.

A GAME OF CHESS

Simcha Bunam, the Zaddik of Parsischa, sought to cause a sinner to improve his ways. He invited him to a game of chess and, while playing, the Zaddik made an obviously wrong move. The man was about to take advantage of the error, but the Zaddik asked him to excuse the mistake. Soon the Zaddik made another wrong move, and this time his opponent refused to overlook it. The Zaddik turned to him and said:

"You refuse to condone two wrong moves in a game of chess, yet you expect the Lord to pardon you regardless of the number of your own transgressions."

The sinner was stricken with remorse and promised to improve his conduct.

DOING A GOOD DEED

The rabbi of Kotzk said: "There are three ways in which a man can go about performing a good deed. If he says 'I shall do it soon,' the method is poor. If he says 'I am ready to do it now,' the method is of average quality. If he says 'I am doing it,' the method is praiseworthy."

ON TRUTH

Rabbi Mordecai of Tzernobil said: "If you wish to acquire the habit of truthfulness make it a point, when you catch yourself telling a falsehood, to say unashamedly: 'I have just been guilty of a lie.' In this manner you will speedily discipline your tongue."

ON READERS

There are two kinds of readers of serious books. One is like the man who squeezes wine grapes with his fingertips. He secures only the watery juice from the ends of the grapes and, inasmuch as it does not ferment, he complains that the grapes are poor. This type of reader glances hurriedly at the pages of a volume and finds no merit in the writings.

The other kind of reader is like the man who squeezes out the full juice from the grapes. It ferments and turns into pleasing wine. This type of reader delves deeply into the words he is reading and finds delight in thoughts they convey.

ON LOVE

Moses Leib, the Chasidic rabbi of Sassev, declared to his disciples:

"I learned how we must truly love our neighbors from the conversation between two villagers which I overheard. The first said: 'Tell me friend, do you love me?'

The second villager replied, 'I love you deeply.'

The first thought and then asked: 'Do you know, my friend, what gives me pain?'

The second replied: 'How can I, pray, know what gives you pain?

'If you do not know what gives me pain,' quietly replied the first neighbor, 'how can you say that you truly love me?'

"Understand, my sons," continued Rabbi Moses Leib, "to love—to truly love, means to know what brings pain to your fellow human beings."

98

As you can see, the fact that the Torah has endured through the ages can be attributed to the dedicated teachers in Israel. Indeed, many of them sacrificed their lives for this ideal because they realized that passing on the precepts of the Torah from generation to generation was vital to the very survival of the Jewish people. In the *Musaf* service of Yom Kippur there is a prayer dedicated to ten martyrs, saintly teachers who lived during the reign of Hadrian. They had incurred the hatred of the government by defying an imperial edict which prohibited organizing schools for the study of Torah, and each was made to suffer a different type of extremely cruel death. In other times, other great teachers have suffered similarly. In every generation, therefore, we owe a particular debt to those who keep the life-blood of Judaism flowing by teaching us the word of the Lord.

chapter 8

BOOK OF THE PEOPLE

God said to man: "My light, My Torah, is in your hand, and your light, your soul, is in My hand. If you will guard My light, I will guard your light, but if you will extinguish My light, I will extinguish your light."

Make thy books thy
companions;
Let thy shelves be thy gardens.
Bask in their paradise and
gather their fruit.

JUDAH IBN TIBBON

BOOK OF THE PEOPLE

The Bible, the repository of Jewish Law, sometimes referred to as the Pentateuch, includes the Five Books of Moses. The five books are: Genesis, Exodus, Leviticus, Numbers and Deuteronomy. Study of the Torah is the obligation of every Jew, for the Torah is the embodiment of Jewish thought and vision, the medium of Divine speech and human love. There can be no Judaism without Torah. And the Jewish claim to the gratitude of the world is based on the fact that we have given mankind the word of God, the Bible. Morris Rosenfeld, in an inspired mood, wrote:

> Is it a book, a world, a heaven?
> Are those words, or flames, or shining stars,
> Or burning torches, or clouds of fire
> What is it, I ask ye—The Bible?
>
> Who inspired those infinite truths?
> Who spoke through the mouth of the Prophet?
> Who mapped out the highways of ages,
> The glorious lines of the Scriptures?
>
> Who planted the flowers of wisdom
> In this sacred soil of the angels?
> O dream of eternity—Bible—
> O Light that is all and forever.

104

It has been said that the Bible is the textbook of Judaism. It is not the legacy of the wise alone. It does not belong only to the scholar, the priest, or the rich. It is the inheritance of the entire congregation of Israel. Anyone who thirsts for the knowledge of God may come and drink of the living waters of the Torah.

The Bible is known as a charter of peace, a charter of freedom, a charter of the future life of mankind. "From century to century," wrote Israel Zangwill, "even unto this day, through the fairest regions of civilization, the Bible dominates existence. Its vision of life moulds states and societies. Its Psalms are more popular in every country than the poems of the nation's own poets. Besides this one book, all other literature seem 'trifles light as air.'"

The Pentateuch is the chief source of what we know about the faith and the earliest history of the Jewish people. So precious is it to us that we divide it into fixed weekly portions and read one each Sabbath in the year, with special readings on holy days. Years ago, Ben Azzi wrote, "I string together like pearls the words of the Pentateuch, the Prophets and the Hagiographa, and they are as thrilling as on the day when they were revealed in flame on Sinai."

When Rabbi Morris Adler was asked, "What is Torah?" he answered:

"Torah is the attempt of a people covenanted with God to fulfill its obligations. It is the quest of the mind for understanding and of the spirit for fulfillment. Torah is the ladder by which the Jew seeks to ascend to God. It is the bridge he builds between himself and humanity. Torah is the worship of God by means of study. It is the prayer of the mind. It is the science which seeks to discover the laws of the moral universe and thus it deals with the realities that lie above and beyond the world of visible nature. It is man's pilgrimage through life in search of himself. Torah is the shrine which the Jew builds of thought and feeling and aspiration. It is the tree of life and in its shade alone can the Jew find completeness, peace and serenity. The Torah is truly the foundation of life. In it is protection greater than is in fortresses."

105

It is important to understand that when a Jew says, "Let us study Torah," he is not necessarily referring only to the Five Books of Moses, but could mean the Prophets, Mishna, Talmud, or any of the sacred writings—all of which are considered part of the Torah. To the Jewish student, one of the most important works is the Talmud. This contains the teachings of the Rabbis, who devoted their time to the study of the Bible and sought to explain it, thus spreading knowledge among the people.

The Talmud, enabled the Jews not only to live as a people, but even to thrive. The word Talmud comes from the Hebrew root word *lamod* to learn.

Massive in size and written in Aramaic, the Talmud has long baffled many. At first, its teachings were handed down orally, from teacher to pupil. This is why it is called the Oral Law. When the number of teachings had grown large, efforts were made by various rabbis to codify them in the form of a book. It is said that Hillel, Akiba and Rabbi Meir, each a famous teacher, made such attempts. But the first one who really succeeded was the great teacher, Rabbi Judah ha-Nassi. His work was called the *Mishnah*, a term derived from *shanah*, which means to repeat or study. There are six main sections to the Mishnah, which in turn are subdivided into chapters and individual paragraphs.

The Talmud embodies the civil and religious laws and traditions of the Jewish people, and represents the thoughts of many generations of rabbis and sages of Israel. It is a record of the discussions and the religious decisions of the Rabbis extending over many centuries. It includes the prayers, customs, laws, legends, history and ideals of the Jewish people. For thousands of years, the Jews studied the Talmud and have guided their lives by its teachings.

In the Talmud you will find much profound wisdom, sparkling epigrammatic wit, and many pertinent parables, legends and anecdotes, each stating a definite lesson or truth. It covers every possible subject concerning life. Heinrich Graetz, in his *History of the Jews,* wrote, "The Talmud preserved and promoted the religious and moral life of Judaism; it held out a banner to the communities scattered in all corners of the earth, and protected them from schism and sectarian divisions, it acquainted subse-

106

quent generations with the history of their nation; finally, it produced a deep intellectual life which preserved the enslaved and lit for them the torch of science."

The Talmud is, in effect, a supplement to the Pentateuch. It consists of two distinct parts: the *Mishna* and the *Gemara*, the commentary. In the Talmud one can find the fundamental law of all human and social economy. It appeals to the imagination and the feelings; above all, it challenges the mind. As one studies its keenly reasoned arguments, it immediately becomes apparent that the Jewish religion is not merely dogma.

There are six main sections in the Talmud and they are called *Sedarim*, "Orders," because each section represents an orderly arrangement of the laws on its particular subject. They are: *Zeraim, Moed, Nashim, Nezikin, Kodoshim, Toharot.*

Zeraim deals with agriculture.
Moed deals with the Sabbath and the festivals.
Nashim discusses marriage and divorce and phases of family life.
Nezikin deals with civil and criminal law.
Kodoshim discusses holy things, such as Temple service.
Toharot deals with questions of ritual purity.

The Talmud is devoted mostly to two kinds of teachings: laws and moral lessons. The parts that contain the laws are called *Halacha*, and those containing moral lessons are called *Agada*. The *Halacha* and the *Agada* have the same objective: to help Jewish men and women live pure, upright and noble lives.

The following pages offer a small sample of the 2,500,000 words that make up the Talmud, which represents the spiritual creativeness of more than two thousand scholars over a period of nearly ten centuries.

WHO IS A WISE MAN?

Says the Mishna on the subject of wisdom:

Who is a wise man? He who learns from all men.

He who is ashamed to ask, will never learn.

One who spends the night studying, it is a good omen, but one who spends the night in conversation only, it is a bad omen for him.

A wise man speaks not before those who surpass him in wisdom and years.

A wise man interrupts not another in his speech.

A wise man addresses himself to first things first.

If a man has knowledge, he has all things; if he has no knowledge, he has nothing.

If a man does not go after wisdom, wisdom will not come to him.

If you interrupt your studies for one day, it will take you two to regain what you have lost.

To acquire knowledge and not impart it to others may be compared to a beautiful plant flourishing in the untraversed desert, where no one is benefited by its existence.

Unless a man clearly understands and inwardly digests what he studies, let him read ever so much; he can only be compared to a box well filled with books. Like that box, he carries books within him, and like the box he is none the wiser for it.

GEMS OF WISDOM

A scholar once said of the Talmud: "It passes from myth to morality, from legend to logic, from grave to gay, from lively to severe topics." And he might have added that the gems of wisdom in its pages are as applicable to life today as they were to society thousands of years ago. Here are some examples:

The mob hath many heads, but no brains.

Unwelcome news is always soon enough heard.

Unskillful workmen quarrel with their tools.

He who swells in prosperity will be sure to shrink in adversity.

Speak well of your friend. Of your enemy say nothing.

By learning to obey, you will learn how to command.

If you have to sign your name on a blank piece of paper, sign at the very top so that nothing may be written above your signature.

Deliberate slowly, execute promptly, avoid anger; cool reflection can only take place when you are calm. Defer not to evening what the morning may accomplish.

Promise little, and do much.

Some are very busy, and yet do nothing.

Economy is itself a great income.

Ready money is ready medicine.

Charity should begin at home, but not end there.

He gives little who gives with a frown. He gives much who gives with a smile.

Of the friends you have, cling to those who censure you, and avoid those who praise you.

Keep an inventory of your friends, rather than of your goods.

A faithful friend is the medicine of life.

He who gossips about others will also gossip about you.

Avoid a slanderer as you would a scorpion.

No pains, no profit.

Some act with their hands, others with their tongues.

He that would thrive must rise at five.

Many who possess much enjoy but little.

Silence is the fence around wisdom.

Give your tongue more holidays than your hands or eyes.

Vows made in storms are forgotten in calms.

He that lives upon hopes will die starving.

Cut not down the tree that shades you.

Few are they who see their own faults.

A fault is made worse by endeavoring to conceal it.

Study to be useful, rather than diverting.

We never know the worth of water till the well is dry.

Do not confine your children to your own learning, for they were born in another age.

Empty vessels make the most noise.

Without law, civilization perishes.

A word is like the bee. It has honey and a sting.

The shortest answer is doing the thing.

While the fool speaks, the wise man thinks.

HONOR THY PARENTS

Nathina was a wealthy diamond merchant who owned a certain diamond which the High Priest desired for his *Ephod* (a priestly vestment worn by the High Priest). He had placed a price of sixty myriads on this diamond.

When the High Priest's messengers called at Nathina's home to purchase the diamond, they were met at the door by his son, Damah. They stated their mission and offered the price asked, but the son shook his head.

"My father is asleep," said Damah, "and I dare not disturb him."

Knowing how much their master desired the diamond, they increased their offer, but the son still shook his head. So they went away. The next day they returned, and when the son again met them at the door they offered him a fabulous sum for the diamond.

"My friends," said the young man, "the diamond shall be yours for sixty myriads. Yesterday, when you called my father was asleep and the key to the safe, where the diamond is kept, was under his pillow. I would not disturb my father in his rest for any sum to obtain it for you. You may now have the diamond for the amount first asked by my father, as I do not desire profit merely because I honored my father."

Says the Talmud further on the subject of honoring one's parents:

There are many ways in which honor is to be shown to parents. If they have a certain corner in the room which they prefer or a certain chair on which they sit, these are not to be used even when not used by them. They must not be contradicted, and attention is to be shown them in every possible way.

A child must not only love and honor his parents while they are living, but must love them and respect them after they are dead.

Honor thy father and thy mother by attending to their wants. Give them food and drink and even tie their shoes if they are unable to do so themselves.

A child who has prospered must share his prosperity with his parents. He should not live in greater luxury than they and must not permit them to live in poverty while he enjoys wealth.

He who honors his father and mother enjoys the fruit in his life, and stores up a treasure for the future.

THE DIGNITY OF HONEST LABOR

A wealthy landowner once employed a great number of men to fill up a large gully on his estate.

One of the workmen, on looking into the vast depths of the ravine said: "This is so deep, we shall never be able to fill it." So he gave up the task. However, the others said: "It matters not how deep it is. We should be happy to have honest and useful work to do and, by perseverance, we shall eventually be able to fill it."

Says the Talmud further on the subject of honest labor:

If thou art engaged by the day, do thy work to the best of thy ability and think of naught else.

The dignity of labor is great. It honors man.

There can be no indignity in earning an honest wage, whatever the work may be.

111

A man supported by others, be they even his own parents or his own children, cannot feel that joy in life which the man feels who supports himself by the work of his own hands.

BE NOT GREEDY

Mar Ukba was a very kind and charitable man. There was a poor man in his neighborhood whom he wished to help, but he desired to do so in such a manner that the poor man would not know who his benefactor was, because it is written in the Talmud, "He who gives charity in secret is greater than Moses."

Very early each morning, Mar Ukba would go to the poor man's home, slide four coins under his door, and leave stealthily before anyone could see him.

One day the poor man said to himself, "I will arise early and see who it is that is so kind to me and perhaps I can induce him to give me more."

The next day, when Mar Ukba approached the house, the poor man opened the door. Mar Ukba, rather than put him to shame by dispensing charity to him in public, turned and ran and never approached that house again. Hence was the poor man punished because he was not content to accept what was given him.

Says the Talmud further on the subject of greed:

Crave not for the crown of kings, for thy crown may be greater than their crown.

BE NOT BLINDED BY SILVER

There was once a wealthy man who was very miserly and who was never known to give to charity or help the needy in any way. One day, his rabbi sent for him and asked if he would not contribute to the assistance of a certain very poor family greatly in need of food and medicine, but he refused.

112

The rabbi then handed him a mirror and said: "Look into this mirror and tell me what you see."

"This is no different from any other mirror," he said, "I see my face in it but nothing else."

"Now," replied the rabbi, "look through that window and tell me what you see."

The wealthy man looked through the window as the rabbi bade him and said, "I see men and women about their daily duties. Now I see two lovers walking by, engrossed in each other. And there, across the way, is a group of children playing. But why do you ask that?"

"You have answered your own question," replied the rabbi. "When you looked through the window you looked at life, but when you looked into the mirror you saw only yourself. A mirror is only a plain piece of glass, like the window through which you looked, but it is coated on the back with a layer of silver. Just as this bit of silver on the back of the glass has concealed your view of life and enabled you to see only your own countenance, so has your silver, your wealth, concealed all else from your sight and narrowed your view so that you can see and think only of yourself. This silver has shut out from your view and thoughts all the worthwhile things of life."

As the rabbi spoke the rich man hung his head in shame. "I have been blinded by a bit of silver, but thanks to you I now see the light."

RESPECT THY NEIGHBOR'S PROPERTY

Once while walking along a road, Rabbi Joshua noticed a worn path which led across an adjoining field. It appeared that this would shorten his journey considerably, so he started across the path. He had not gone far when he met a little girl who said: "Sir, thou art walking in our field."

"Is this not a trodden path?" asked the rabbi.

"Yes," she exclaimed, "such robbers as thou art have made it a trodden path."

Says the Talmud further on the subject of respecting a neighbor's property:

Destroy not the property of thy neighbor.
Thy neighbor's property must be as sacred as thine own.
Offend not thy neighbor.
Be mindful of the feelings of others.

A TREE IS KNOWN BY ITS FRUIT

"Why is it that the sound of thy flowing waters cannot be heard even a short distance from thy shores?" asked all the other rivers of the Euphrates River.

"It is not necessary that my waters be heard," replied the Euphrates. "My deeds, my fruitful shores, speak for me."

The rivers then asked of the Tigris river, "Why is it that the tumult and splashing of thy waters may be heard for such a great distance?"

"Because," replied the noisy Tigris, "it is necessary that my current rush with tumultous rumble and clamor so people may hear and know how important I am."

Likewise did the trees of the forest ask of the fruit trees, "Why is it that the rustling of thy leaves may not be heard at a distance?"

"Because," replied the fruit trees, "our fruits testify for us. It is not necessary that we attract attention by the rustling of our leaves. Now we shall ask a question of thee, "Why do thy leaves rustle constantly?"

"That," answered the forest trees, "is because we must call the attention of others to our presence."

Says the Talmud further on this subject:

Man is to be judged by his deeds, not by his words.
As a tree is known by its fruit, so is man by his works.

114

A GOOD WIFE IS PRICELESS

When Abraham brought Sarah into Egypt he is said to have hidden her in a box in order that no one should see her beauty. When tax payment was demanded by the customs officer at the boundary line, Abraham said he was ready to pay.

"Thou bringest clothes?" asked the custom house officer.

"I will pay for clothes," replied Abraham.

"Thou bringest gold?" asked the officer.

"I will pay for gold," returned Abraham.

"Thou bringest silk?" the officer asked.

"I will pay for silk," he said.

"Thou bringest pearls?" the officer continued.

"I will pay for pearls," replied Abraham. "A good wife is more precious than silk, pearls or gold."

Says the Talmud further on the subject of a good wife:

All the blessings of a household come through the wife, therefore should her husband honor her.

He who loves his wife as himself and honors her more than himself, will train his children properly.

Who is to be considered rich?

"Everyone who enjoys his riches," replied Rabbi Meier.

"Everyone who has a hundred vineyards and a hundred fields and a hundred slaves to labor therein," said Rabbi Tarphon.

But Rabbi Akiba said, "He is richest of all, who has a wife who is becoming in all her acts."

There is another great body of Jewish literature, developed by the Rabbis as they explained and studied the Bible with the people, which is called the Midrash. This is very much like certain parts of the Talmud and contains homilies, stories and interpretations of Jewish law and ethics. Homilies based on legal teachings are known as *Midrash Halachah*. Homilies based on ethical and narrative teachings are known as *Midrash Agada*. The word Midrash is derived from the Hebrew root, *dorosh*, meaning to search out and investigate. The best known and most

115

important of the *midrashim* were compiled about one thousand years ago and are called the *Midrash Rabba,* the Great Midrash.

The following stories are illustrations of what may be found in the Midrash.

IS THIS MAN?

Rabbi Joshua ben Levi visited Rome. He was astonished to behold the magnificence of the buildings, the tremendous statues covered with tapestry to protect them from the heat of summer and the cold of winter. As he was admiring the beauty of Roman art, a beggar tugged at his sleeve and pleaded for a crust of bread. The rabbi looked again at the statues, and turning to the man in rags, cried out: "O Lord, here are statues of stone covered with expensive garments. Here is a man, created in Thine own image, covered with rags. A civilization that pays more attention to statues than to men shall surely perish."

THEY PLANTED FOR ME

Emperor Hadrian, passing near Tiberias in Galilee, noticed an old man digging a large trench in order to plant some fig trees. "If you had properly used the morning of your life," remarked Hadrian, "you would not now have to work so hard in the evening of your days."

"I have not wasted my early days, nor will I neglect the evening of my life. Let God do what He thinks best," was the reply of the old man.

"How old are you?" asked the Emperor.

"A hundred years," was the prompt reply.

"What!" exclaimed Hadrian, "a hundred years old and you still plant trees! Do you hope, then, to ever enjoy the fruits of your labor?"

"Mighty Emperor," rejoined the hoary-headed man, "yes, I do hope. If God wills it, I may even eat the fruit of these very trees; if not, my children will. Have not my forefathers planted trees for me, and shall I not do the same for my children?"

Hadrian, pleased with the honest man's reply, said, "Well, old man, if you ever live to see the fruit of these trees, let me know it."

The old man did live long enough to see the fruits of his industry. The trees bore excellent fruit. As soon as they were ripe, he gathered the choicest figs, put them in a basket, and marched off toward the Emperor's palace. Hadrian happened to look out one of the windows. Seeing a man bent with age, with a basket on his shoulders, standing near the gate, he ordered him to be admitted to his presence.

"May it please your Majesty," replied the man, "to recollect seeing once a very old man planting some trees, and you desired him, if ever he should gather fruit, to let you know. I am that old man and this is the fruit of those very trees. May it please you graciously to accept them as a tribute of gratitude for your Majesty's condescension."

Hadrian ordered that the basket be emptied of the fruit and filled with gold, and he gave it to the old man as a present.

THE BEST LAWYER

A man had three friends. Two of them he loved dearly, but the other he lightly esteemed. It happened one day that the king commanded his presence at court, which greatly alarmed him, and he wished to procure a lawyer. Accordingly, he went to the two friends whom he loved. One flatly refused to accompany him; the other offered to go with him as far as the king's gate, but no further. In his extremity he called upon the third friend, whom he least esteemed, and he not only went willingly with him, but so ably defended him before the king that he was acquitted.

In like manner every man has three friends when death summons him to appear before his Creator. His first friend, whom he loves most, namely, his money, cannot go with him a single step; his second, relations and neighbors can only accompany him to the grave, but cannot defend him before the Judge; while his third friend, whom he does not highly esteem, his good works, goes with him before the King and obtains his acquittal.

There are also other great works, which are part of the great literature of our people, relating to the various questions of

117

religion and conduct. Such men as Saadya, Maimonides, Rashi, Abarbanel and a large number of other rabbis have added to our literature from age to age.

If we are to understand our religion thoroughly, we must keep on studying the Bible and all other teachings carefully. Moses Ibn Ezra advised: "If you do not want to bear the light burden of education, you will have to bear the heavy burden of ignorance."

To the Jew, the Torah is a source of inspiration and wisdom. It helps bring God into his every day existence; it is the essence of his faith. No Judaism can survive without the Torah and no Jew can make a meaningful contribution to the perpetuation of his people without steadily increasing his knowledge of the sacred writings.

chapter 9

THE SABBATH

"Six days shalt thou labor and do all thy
work; but the seventh day is Sabbath unto
the Lord thy God."

THE SABBATH

The greatest gift the Almighty gave to His people was the Sabbath, which he established by His own example: "For in six days the Lord worked in creating the universe; and He rested on the seventh day." The importance attached to the *Shabbat*, the day of rest, is further demonstrated by the fact that the fourth commandment of the Ten Commandments demands: "Remember to consecrate the Sabbath." As has been often pointed out, the Sabbath was not created for the sake of the weekdays; the weekdays were made for the sake of the Sabbath. The Sabbath is not an interlude but the climax of living.

A legend relates that at the time when God was giving the Torah to Israel, He said to them: "My children, if you accept the Torah and observe My *mitzvot*, I will give you for all eternity a most precious gift."

"What is this precious gift," asked Israel of the Almighty.

"The world to come," was the reply.

"Show us in this world an example of the world to come," requested Israel.

"A good example of the world to come," replied God, "is the Sabbath." According to the Talmud, the Sabbath is *me'en olam haba*, a slight taste of the world to come.

The Sabbath and the Jew were united many centuries ago. It is a strong institution which arose and engraved itself upon the hearts of Israel generation after generation. It stimulated joy in

122

the midst of sorrow. It inspired hope, banished fear and healed broken hearts.

The Jew, with his love of home-life and his devotion to study, has shown how the Sabbath can be made not only a day of respite from work but a positive factor in human well-being. On the Sabbath we are reminded that man was not created for work alone; that one day should be set aside for rest and reflection, devoid of all thoughts of business.

Today, it is common practice to set aside a day for rest. However, when the Jew ordained the Sabbath it was the first time in human history that a religious faith set aside one day of every week for rest, for communion with God and for self improvement. The Jew went even further. He set aside this same day of rest for his slaves and servants as well.

Abraham J. Heschel, in his writings, has caught the beauty of the spirit of the Sabbath: "The world has our hands, but our soul belongs to Someone Else. Six days a week we seek to dominate the world, on the seventh day we try to dominate the self. . . . To set apart one day a week for freedom, a day on which we would not use the instruments which have been so easily turned into weapons of destruction, a day for being with ourselves, a day of detachment from the vulgar, of independence of external obligations, a day on which we stop worshipping the idols of technical civilization, a day on which we use no money, a day of armistice in the economic struggle with our fellow men and the forces of nature—is there any institution that holds out a greater hope for man's progress than the Sabbath?

"In the tempestuous ocean of time and toil there are islands of stillness where man may enter a harbor and reclaim his dignity. The island is the seventh day, the Sabbath, a day of detachment from things, instruments and practical affairs as well as of attachment to the spirit."

Three acts of God denoted the seventh day: He rested on it, He blessed it, and He hallowed it. Our great Rabbis indicate the sacredness and importance of the Sabbath by declaring that "if Israel would strictly observe two consecutive Sabbaths, redemption would follow as a result thereof." In other words, the Jewish

Sabbath is designed to give men peaceful hours, hours completely directed to self improvement. The Rabbis taught that the Sabbath was made for man; man was not created for the Sabbath. "Sanctify the Sabbath by choice meals, by beautiful garments; delight your soul with pleasure," said the Lord, "and I will reward you for this very pleasure."

It is no wonder our great sages stated that on *Shabbat* each individual has two souls, since to the Jew the Sabbath is a day of happiness wherein a general sense of exhilaration prevails. The Sabbath is no time for personal anxiety, nor for any activity that might dampen the spirit of joy. Fasting (except on Yom Kippur, which is called the Sabbath of Sabbaths), mourning and demonstrations of grief are forbidden.

The continuing and unique value of the Sabbath to the Jew in modern society was made vividly clear some years ago by Cyrus Adler:

> "If I were asked to single out one of the great historical institutions more essential for our preservation than all others, I would not hesitate to declare that it is the observance of the Sabbath. Without this, the home and the synagogue, the Festivals and the Holy Days, the language and the history of our people would gradually disappear. If the Sabbath will be maintained by those who have observed it, and will be restored to those who have abandoned it, then the permanence of Judaism is assured. To all who are prosperous, the question of the observance of the Sabbath involves the sacrifice of a luxury, nothing more. . . . Every Jew who has it within his power should aid the effort to restore the Sabbath to the man from whom it has been taken away. No deeds of charity or philanthropy, no sacrifices of time or fortune made by any Jew, at all equals in beneficent result the expenditure of time and money looking toward the re-establishment of the Jewish Sabbath among the Jewish people. No amount of prating about morals will ever take the place of rooted habits ruthlessly plucked out."

124

In the days of old, as well as today, great preparations were made for the Sabbath. Everything was immaculately cleaned and meticulously prepared. Extra delicacies were made. It was considered a *mitzvah* to wear better clothes than during the week and to look particularly neat on the Sabbath. Our Rabbis felt it was their duty to do something special for this sacred day. One polished candlesticks; another prepared the fish. The women of the household earned a special mitzvah by baking *chalah*.

While the father is preparing to go to the synagogue, the mother sets the table with her finest silverware and linen and places two *chalot* on the table. A special cloth (symbolizing the manna from heaven that was covered with dew) is placed over the *chalot*. Fifteen minutes before sunset the mother kindles the Sabbath lights. The prevailing custom is to light two candles, though many light one candle, in addition, for each member of the family.

Various opinions are offered for the lighting of Sabbath candles. Rashi states that no full meal should be served in darkness. Maimonides claims that to light the home is a pleasure and one should seek pleasure on the Sabbath.

The father, upon returning from the synagogue service, leads his family in singing *Shalom Aleichem*, an ode in honor of angels. According to legend, on Sabbath eve, two angels accompany a man from the synagogue to his home. As they come into the house and find it lit and the family in a happy mood, one angel says: "May next Sabbath be like this!" And the other angel answers, "Amen." Following the singing of *Shalom Aleichem*, the father chants *Eishes Cha-yil*, a song honoring his wife.

To consecrate the Sabbath, father and son recite the *kiddush* over a goblet of wine, as it is written: "Remember the Sabbath." The Sabbath *kiddush* expresses gratitude to the Lord for making Israel worthy of His favor, as first expressed by Israel's deliverance from Egypt, and for the Divine gift of the Sabbath. Then the meal begins with the family washing and the father pronouncing *hamotzi*, the blessing for bread, over the two *chalot*. These symbolize the Lord's command to the Israelites that they gather twice

125

as much manna on Friday as on any other day. During the meal *zmiros,* songs praising the Sabbath, are sung.

Some time ago, there appeared "Ten Commandments For Friday Evening." A careful study of them will give you a clear idea of what should and should not be done on *Sabbath.*

TEN COMMANDMENTS FOR THE SABBATH

1. I am the Sabbath that frees you from bondage and from mundane pursuits and lifts you towards life's highest values.
2. You shall have no secular appointments on the Sabbath for it is a day of spiritual rest.
3. You shall not take the name of the Sabbath in vain. Keep it holy.
4. Remember the Sabbath for it has been given to you for worship and cultural pursuit.
5. Honor your father and mother by joining them at Sabbath services with unfailing regularity.
6. You shall not kill the Sabbath spirit by following alien activities on this holy day.
7. You shall not be unfaithful to Jewish tradition by banishing Sabbath candles and *kiddush* from your home.
8. You shall not steal the precious hours that belong to the synagogue and Judaism by using them for unworthy, unspiritual pursuits.
9. You shall not bear false witness against fellow Jews by showing disrespect for the Sabbath.
10. You shall not covet the way of life of those who act as if Judaism has no meaning and no message for the modern world.

126

On Saturday morning, after the synagogue services, *kiddush* is again recited and another delicious meal is served. During the afternoon there is a *Mincha* service and a third delicious meal is served. After the evening prayer, *M'ariv*, the *havdalah* ceremony is performed. *Havdalah* means separation; it separates the holiness of the Sabbath from the usual routine of the week-days. It is recited over wine, beer or milk, and during the ceremony a braided wax candle is lit and spices are smelled. Like the *kiddush*, it is a home ceremony, marking the close of the Sabbath and the return of the week days.

It might be pointed out that a great deal of Judaism's most beautiful ceremonies do not take place in the synagogue. They are performed in the home, with the family, helping to make the home a *mikdash m'at*, a small sanctuary.

It is said that "had Judaism brought into the world *only* the Sabbath, it would thereby have proved itself a producer of joy and a promoter of peace." This is what C. G. Montefiore pointed out when he wrote: "The Sabbath is one of the glories of our humanity. For if to labor is noble, of our own free will to pause in that labor which may lead to success, to money, to fame, is nobler still. To dedicate one day a week to rest and to God, this is the prerogative and the privilege of man alone."

In truth, the Sabbath was the first step on the road which led to the abrogation of slavery. "What was created on the Sabbath day?" asks the Midrash. Seven words make up the answer: "Contentment, peace of mind, and physical rest."

The Sabbath occupies a large portion of Hebrew literature and learning. The Talmud and the writings of our great scholars deal with Sabbath observance, and the holiness of the day.

Rabbi Yudan said: "According to the ordinary custom of the world, the master tells his servants: 'Work for me six days and one day shall be for yourselves.' God, however, says: 'Work for yourselves six days, and for Me one day.'"

Rabbi Chanina said: "A joyous spirit should be a rule on the Sabbath day." Only with difficulty was permission

127

granted to console mourners or visit the sick on the Sabbath day.

Break the Sabbath so that a sick man may live to keep many Sabbaths.

Danger to life takes precedence over the sanctity of the Sabbath.

The Sabbath is a foretaste of heaven, so pure and exalted is the happiness it offers to the careworn spirit.

The housewife should kindle the Sabbath candles with a joyous heart and good will, for it is a great privilege accorded to her. It brings her the merit of holy sons, who will be Lights of the World in Torah, and who will increase peace on earth. It also merits her to give long life unto her husband. Therefore she should be careful in the observance of this *Mitzvah*.

In the Zohar we read: For the commandment is a lamp, and the teaching is light. The Sabbath lamp is the commandment for women, and the learning of Torah is a light unto men. When the wife prepares all that is proper for the Sabbath, and the husband learns or teaches the Torah, both give forth a light.

Rabbi Meier Shalom of Porissov said: "If we avoid the thought of money on the Sabbath, we shall not lack it on week days. Sabbath is a day of rest. Abstain from hard work on it, even in the service of the Lord."

The Sassover Rabbi narrated the following parable: A man invited an important personage for a Sabbath meal and prepared a sumptuous feast for him. Later, however, he changed his mind and did not call for his guest. In similar fashion, many persons make elaborate preparations to welcome the Sabbath, but the atmosphere at their table is the same as on a weekday, and no Sabbath hymns are chanted.

One version of the Decalogue reads: "Remember the Sabbath day." The other version reads: "Observe the Sabbath day." Remember it a little while before it arrives, and observe it once it is here. Too often it is the Jew, whose introduction of the day of rest has won him the appreciation and admiration of non-Jews, who himself fails to understand and enjoy the beauty of the Sabbath.

Let this not be true of you!

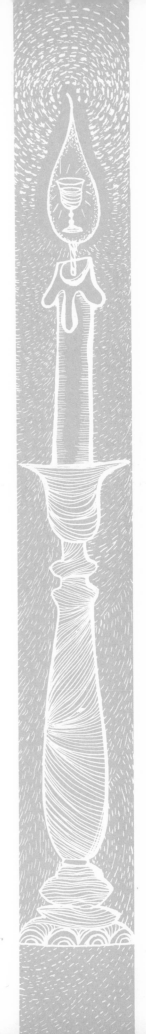

chapter 10

THE DAYS OF AWE

Once during the penitential season, Rabbi
Levi Isaac was ill. As he lay in bed, he
prayed: "Merciful Lord! I am weak and
unable to arise to recite the lengthy
Selichos prayers of forgiveness. You are
strong and Your penitential prayers are
brief; therefore, say: 'I forgive.'"

THE DAYS OF AWE

Before we can begin a meaningful discussion of the Days of Awe, or of any of the other occasions that mark the Hebrew calendar, we must know something about the calendar itself.

First of all, the Hebrew calendar calculates the day from evening to evening, following the example set in Genesis: "And there was evening and there was morning, one day." Thus, the day includes both day and night, covering twenty-four hours from one evening to the next. The evening begins when three stars can be plainly seen in the skies; the day begins and ends when the stars have come out.

The Hebrew calendar, unlike most secular calendars, which are based on the rotation of the earth around the sun (and are therefore known as "solar" calendars), is based on the rotation of the moon around the earth and is referred to as the "lunar" calendar. Since it takes the moon twenty-nine and a half days to run its course around the earth and it would be inconvenient in practice to have one half a day belong to one month and the other half of the same day to another month, the Jewish month has either twenty-nine or thirty days. This makes the lunar year about eleven days shorter than the solar year, so every two or three years there is a leap-year which wipes out the difference by the addition of a thirteenth month, known as the Second Adar.

In days of old, the appearance of the new moon, which marks the beginning of the month, was a half holiday. In ancient Palestine, the new moon was fixed by actual observation. To avoid confusion, the chief of the Sanhedrin and two other members of the High Court were given the right to announce the appearance of the new moon. With the passage of time, however, it became more and more difficult to depend on observation for fixing of the new moon. Calculation, based on the science of astronomy, therefore took the place of observation, and the calendar was fixed for all time. Thus, the Jews, no matter how far apart they lived, knew that they all followed the same calendar and were able to observe their Holy Days at the same time. The permanent calendar was fixed by Hillel II, head of the academy in Tiberias, about the year 360 C. E.

When the Jews lived in Babylon they adopted names for their months from the Babylonian calendar. Those names, which we use to this day, are:

1. Nisan	7. Tishri
2. Iyar	8. Cheshvan
3. Sivan	9. Kislev
4. Tamuz	10. Tevet
5. Av	11. Shevat
6. Elul	12. Adar

The first month, Nisan, is the month in which the children of Israel were delivered from Egypt, and we are told in Exodus: "This month shall be unto you the beginning of months; it shall be the first month of the year for you."

In practice, however, the Hebrew New Year is at the beginning of Tishri, the seventh calendar month. It was during Tishri that the world was created.

The following is a list of the leading Jewish Holy Days and their dates:

Nisan	14	Eve of Passover (Pesach)
	15	First Day of Passover
	16	Second Day of Passover
	21	Seventh Day of Passover
Sivan	6	Feast of Pentecost, or (Shavuot)
	7	Second Day of Shavuot
Av	9	Ninth of Av (Tisha B'Av)
Tishri	1	New Year (Rosh Hashanah)
	2	Second Day of Rosh Hashanah
	10	Day of Atonement (Yom Kippur)
	15	First Day of Tabernacles (Sukkot)
	16	Second Day of Sukkot
	22	Eighth Day of Tabernacles
	23	Rejoicing of the Law (Simchat Torah)
Kislev	25	Chanukah—First Day (and lasts for 8 days)

Observance of the Holy Days constitutes an important part of our religious life. If we are careful to keep them in the proper way, they should inspire us with love for our faith, and for the epic history of our people. The Holy Days help us enter deeply into the meaning of our religion and deepen our devotion to God and to Israel.

Examination of the various Jewish festivals discloses that each conveys some particular meaning, and that all have something in common. For example, almost all the Holy Days are meant to give rest from daily work and to turn our thoughts to religion, and the joys and duties it imposes. And, of course, the Holy Days offer a special opportunity for inner reflection, self examination and prayer.

The Solemn Season comes in the fall and lasts ten days. It begins with the Day of the New Year, Rosh Hashanah, and ends ten days later with the Day of Atonement, Yom Kippur. These Holy Days do not refer to any particular event in Jewish history. Rather, their aim is to motivate all of us to examine our conduct in order to determine where we have failed, and to induce us to do better in the future. These days form a season of prayer, penitence and resolution. This is why they are called the Solemn Season, *Yamim Noraim,* or the Ten Days of Penitence, *Aseret Y'mei T'shuvah.*

136

The purpose of the Ten Days of Penitence is clear from their name. They are set aside for prayer and supplication because all earthly life is judged on Rosh Hashanah, and he who returns to God is forgiven on Yom Kippur, as it is written, "And it came to pass about ten days after, that the Lord smote Nabal, so that he died." It has been explained that the ten days are the Ten Days of Penitence, during which the judgment of Nabal was withheld by heaven in the hope that he might repent.

Our Rabbis taught: "Let a man see himself as though he were half-guilty and half-innocent. Happy is he if he does one good deed, for he tips the balance in his favor. If he commits one transgression he tips the balance against himself."

There are twenty-four ways that one can hinder penitence:

1. He who leads a community to sin.
2. He who turns his fellow man from good to evil ways.
3. He who does not prevent his son from acting viciously.
4. He who says, "I will sin and then repent."
5. He who does not repent with the community.
6. He who opposes the dicta of the Sages.
7. He who mocks the commandments.
8. He who despises his teachers.
9. He who hates being admonished.
10. He who curses people in general.
11. He who shares with a thief.
12. He who finds a lost article and does not announce it publicly.
13. He who despoils the poor and the orphaned and the widowed.
14. He who accepts a bribe in order to pervert justice.
15. He who eats a meal where there is not enough for the host.
16. He who makes use of a poor man's pledge.
17. He who looks at a woman he may not marry, and sees her with lust.
18. He who tries to gain honor through disparaging another.

19. He who is suspicious of innocent people.
20. He who hinders a community from fulfilling a commandment.
21. He who commits iniquities in relationship with his fellow man.
22. He who encourages a thief to steal.
23. He who encourages a briber, and leads him to sin.
24. He who is guilty of talebearing and gossip; of evil thought and bad company.

Every man must truly repent before the Day of Atonement. Once, while expounding the customs of Yom Kippur, the Chofetz Chayim, referring to the practice of beating one's heart when the confession of sins is recited, explained: "God does not forgive the sins of one who smites his heart, but He pardons those whose hearts smite them."

Sincere repentance was explained by Rabbi Nachman of Bratzlav in a letter to his son.

"To my beloved son, Rabbi Isaac, may his light shine bright:

"I have this hour received your letter and there is no time to reply to it as it deserves. May God strengthen your heart and waken you on the great and awesome day approaching in peace, that you may merit to be renewed from that time on. And do not let a day be lost without secluding yourself and thinking of the meaning of your life. Into every day get as much of Torah and prayer and good deeds as you can, as much as you can steal from this passing shadow, this vanity of vanities, this vanishing cloud. . . . Remember well that all our days are vanity, yet every man on whatever level he may stand can attain eternal life. There is no time now for any more.

"The words of your father, who seeks your welfare and prays in your behalf,

Nachman of Bratzlav"

ROSH HASHANAH

It is with a feeling of humility and prayer that the Jew approaches the Days of Awe. On the first day of the seventh month, Tishri, we commemorate the creation of the world. "And the Lord spoke unto Moses, saying: 'Speak unto the children of Israel, saying: In the seventh month, in the first day of the month, shall be a solemn rest unto you, a memorial proclaimed with the blast of hours, a holy convocation. Ye shall do no manner of servile work; and ye shall bring an offering made by fire unto the Lord!'"

Rosh Hashanah marks the anniversary of the world. The heavenly court sits in judgment, the books of every man are opened for review and the Divine pen writes. The Lord takes inventory of our deeds to see whether we have profited from another year of existence. The Jew does not spend New Year's day in merrymaking and festivity; he welcomes it in a spirit of reverence.

Rabbi Yochanan said: "Three books are opened on Rosh Hashanah. One for the wholly righteous, one for the wholly wicked and one for the intermediates. The wholly righteous are at once inscribed and sealed in the Book of Life; the wholly wicked are at once inscribed and sealed in the Book of Death; and the intermediates are held suspended from Rosh Hashanah until Yom Kippur. If they are found worthy, they are inscribed for life; if unworthy, they are inscribed for death."

The Jew believes that Rosh Hashanah is a day of decision, when the Almighty sits as Judge and unfolds the record of every person's life, decreeing the destiny of each person for the year just begun. However, the Jew is confident. A man awaiting trial is usually dejected and wears somber garments. Israel, however, is different. On Rosh Hashanah the children of Israel dress in holiday attire and eat a festive-day meal. They are confident of God's mercies.

During the Rosh Hashanah services the great *chasid*, Levi Yitzchak of Berditchev, addressed God thus: "Almighty, Blessed be Thy Name! Why does a Jew pray for a year of sustenance

and plenty? Why does a Jew need money? When a Jew has the means he gives charity to the poor, provides for the education of his children, purchases a choice *Etrog* and *Lulav*, buys beautiful clothing and tasty food to honor Your Sabbath; he also uses money to fulfill the other laws that You have commanded him. If You want the children of Israel to continue to obey Your commandments during the coming year, then You must grant them an abundance of wealth!"

Hebrew literature contains many stories about our devout scholars and incidents relating to certain portions of the holiday prayers, two of which follow:

Rabbi Hurwitz of Stanislav, before reciting "Hear Our Voice," *Shema Kolenu,* during the Rosh Hashanah service, opened the Ark with tears and told the story of a certain king who had an only son whom he reared with tenderness from childhood. His father loved him and raised him in the ways of righteousness. However, the son was a disappointment to his father. The good qualities that had been planted in the boy's youth had grown into ugly ones. His heart had become evil. The king, seeing his son's erring deeds, turned against him and finally was compelled to banish him from his home and country. The son was forced to roam about in strange lands.

He wandered for many years from village to village. His clothes became torn and tattered. His face changed so much that it was difficult to tell that he was the son of the king. After many years of this gypsy life he became homesick. He remembered his father and recalled the palace in which he had lived. His yearning to return to the house of his father became stronger and stronger day by day. Finally, he made up his mind to return home and show his father his great repentance.

When the son came before his father, he cried and begged to be forgiven for the wrongs he had committed. But his father did not recognize him because he had changed so greatly. Then the son began to scream bitterly: "Father, father, if you do not recognize my face, you must remember my voice, for my voice has not changed." Then his father recognized him, and welcomed him into his home again.

140

When Rabbi Hurwitz finished this story, he said: "So it is with us. We are sons to the Lord, our God, the King of kings. The Holy One loved us and desired us, and gave us His sacred Torah that corrects a man and sets him along the straight way of righteousness, but we turned aside and departed from His goodly commandments. We were banished from our land. With the coming of the Sacred Days, we regret our past deeds and return to our Father in heaven, and cry to Him, 'Hear our voice! If You do not recognize our appearance, You must recognize our voice, for we are Your children. Spare and have compassion on us, and receive us and our prayers willingly!'"

In a manuscript by Rabbi Ephraim ben Jacob of Bonn, there is a description of how Rabbi Amnon of Mayence came to compose the prayer, "And We Shall Express the Powerful Sanctity," *U'nsaneh Tokef.*

The story describes Rabbi Amnon as one of the great men of his generation. He was rich and came from a good family. The lords and the archbishop began to demand that Rabbi Amnon convert to their religion. However, he refused to listen to them. One day, after being subjected to continued pressure by the archbishop himself, Rabbi Amnon said, "I wish to take counsel and think about this matter for another three days." He said this to put them off.

However, the moment he left the presence of the archbishop he felt ashamed that he had allowed a word of doubt to leave his lips, as though he needed to take counsel to deny the living God. He returned and would neither eat nor drink. His loved ones came to console him, but he refused to be consoled. "I shall go down to the grave mourning," he said, "because of what I have said." And he wept, and was sad at heart.

On the third day, while Rabbi Amnon was in spiritual pain, the archbishop sent for him. Rabbi Amnon refused to go. He was sent for again and again but refused every request for his presence.

Finally, running out of patience, the archbishop commanded that they bring Rabbi Amnon even against his wishes. When this was done, the archbishop demanded: "What is this, Amnon?

141

Why have you not come when you were summoned? You yourself requested three days in which to take counsel."

And Amnon answered: "I shall pronounce my own sentence. Let the tongue that spoke and lied to you be cut out."

Then the archbishop responded: "No, the tongue I shall not cut out, for it spoke well. But the feet that did not come to me at the time you set I shall lop off, and the rest of the body I shall punish." So the oppressor commanded, and they lopped off Rabbi Amnon's feet and the fingers of his hands. At every finger they asked him, "Will you be converted, Amnon?" And he said, "No."

When they had finished lopping off his fingers, the wicked man ordered that Rabbi Amnon be laid on a shield, with all his fingers at his side, and sent home. He was rightly called Rabbi Amnon, "The Faithful One," for he had faith in the living God and lovingly suffered severe afflictions, simply because of the words he had spoken.

When Rosh Hashanah arrived, Rabbi Amnon asked his relatives to carry him to the House of Prayer just as he was, and to lay him down near the cantor. This they did. And when the cantor came to recite the Sanctification, *Kedusha,* Rabbi Amnon said to him: "Stop! I shall sanctify the great Name of God." And he cried in a loud voice: "And thus may the Sanctification ascend to You . . . we shall express the powerful sanctity of this day." And he continued: "It is true that you are the Judge and Arbiter." He had suffered but the verdict was just. He prayed only that those same fingers of his hands and his feet might rise before God, as well as the memory of the entire incident, and bear witness to his unswerving faith in God. When he concluded, his own end came, and he vanished from the earth before the eyes of all, for God had taken him.

Rosh Hashanah also is known by three other names that reflect its significance:

Yom Teruah—Day of Blowing the Shofar
Yom Zikaron—Day of Remembrance
Yom Hadin—Day of Judgment

142

On the eve of Rosh Hashanah, one goes to the synagogue while it is still daylight. There one finds a holiday spirit. The Ark is draped in white, white covers are on the Torah Scrolls and white cloths are on the reading tables. The white accessories are symbols of forgiveness, as it is said, "Though your sins be as scarlet, they shall become as white as snow." Before leaving the synagogue, the congregants greet one another with the blessing, "May you be inscribed (in the Book of Life) for a good year."

Upon returning home, it is customary to offer the same greeting to the family. The candles are already lit and the table is set with the finest linen and service for a gay holiday meal. After the hands are washed and the *hamotzi* is recited over two *chalot* that are on the table, honey is served as an expression of the wish for a sweet year. Generally, no sour or pickled food is eaten to symbolize the hope that the new year will be free from bitterness, unhappiness and disappointment.

The highlight of the morning service is the blowing of the *Shofar*, the Ram's Horn. This is an affirmative commandment found in the Torah. Saadia Gaon saw ten reasons why the Creator commanded us to blow the *Shofar* on Rosh Hashanah:

1. To remind us of the creation of the world.
2. To remind us of repentance.
3. To remind us of our oath on Mount Sinai.
4. To remind us of the words of our Prophets.
5. To remind us of the destruction of the Temple.
6. To remind us of the binding of Isaac.
7. To remind us to bend our will to the will of the Creator.
8. To remind us of the great Day of Judgment.
9. To remind us of Israel's redemption.
10. To remind us of the revival of the dead.

It is said that all good things come to the Israelites with the blowing of the Shofar. They received the Torah with the sound of the Shofar. They conquered in battle through the blast of the Shofar. They are summoned to repent by the Shofar, and they will be made aware of the Redeemer's arrival through the Great Shofar.

143

On the first afternoon of Rosh Hashanah, or on the second if the first happens to be Saturday or Sunday, orthodox Jews go to a stream or any body of water containing fish—to symbolically rid themselves of their sins. This ceremony is known as *Tashlich,* which means "cast away."

At *Tashlich* the following prayers are recited: The verses from Micah beginning, "Who is a God like unto Thee;" the Thirty-first Psalm and the verse from Isaiah, "They shall not hurt nor destroy in all My holy mountain, for the earth shall be full of the knowledge of the Lord, as the waters cover the sea;" and a prayer composed by Rabbi Chayim Joseph David Azulai.

After the prayers are said, each person shakes out the hems of his clothing three times. This is done to indicate that we are sincere about the casting away of our sins.

YOM KIPPUR

Yom Kippur, the 10th day of Tishri, is the holiest and the most awesome day of the year. It is the climax of the Days of Awe; it is the day of final judgment; Day of Atonement. It is a day of prayer and penitence, a day of entreating the Almighty to forgive all sins committed throughout the past year. It is a day of strict fasting, lasting twenty-four hours, from sunset of the 9th until sunset of the 10th day of Tishri. In the Talmud we find the reason why the 10th of Tishri was selected as Yom Kippur. It was the day on which God forgave Israel for worshipping the golden calf, and it was also the day on which Moses handed down the sacred set of Tablets with the Ten Commandments inscribed on them.

There are three fundamental aspects of Yom Kippur observance: prayer, fasting and charity. Throughout the prayers, over and over again, we make a public confession, *Al Chet,* of the sins which we may have committed through the year. On Yom Kippur God forgives sins committed against Him, but not the wrongs we committed against our fellow men. Only by direct apology and acts of restitution can such wrongs be righted.

Erev Yom Kippur, in many homes, is ushered in by the traditional custom of *Kapporot*. A male takes a rooster, a female, a hen, and recite the prayer, *Bnai-Adam*. They swing the fowl over the head saying: "Be this my atonement." This custom seeks to evoke sincere repentance. The fowl then is properly slaughtered and the meat is used. Generally, the value of the fowl is donated to charity. These days, in fact, the custom of Kapporot is usually observed by donating money to charity rather than by using the fowl.

A sumptuous meal is served before *Kol Nidre*. Afterward, the mother lights candles. It is customary for the father and the mother to bless their children before going to the synagogue. In this blessing the parents pray that the family be sealed for a good life, and that the hearts of their children be firm in the fear of God.

The service begins on this most solemn day with the taking out of two scrolls of the Torah from the Holy Ark, and with the rabbi leading the procession through the synagogue while he chants: "Light is sown for the righteous, and gladness for the upright in heart." This opening prayer characterizes the goals of Judaism: To help man achieve a full life, a life filled with joy and light, for himself and all mankind.

The service continues with the Kol Nidre chant. This is the most stirring and most haunting melody in the entire religious experience of the Jew. The prayer constitutes a plea for release from vows which cannot be kept. It refers to unfulfilled religious commitments, not promises from man to man. To men and women comes the great challenge implicit in the Yom Kippur service: "Behold, I set before thee this day life and good, and death and evil . . . therefore choose good that ye may live."

There is a most popular story told about Rabbi Israel Salanter relating to one Kol Nidre service which he almost failed to attend. The story might be called THE MISSING RABBI.

145

THE MISSING RABBI

The congregation, assembled in the synagogue for the Kol Nidre service scheduled to begin before sunset, waited impatiently for the arrival of their rabbi, Israel Salanter. The sun had already set over the tree tops. The congregants were bewildered for their saintly rabbi always came to the synagogue very early on the eve of the holiest night of the year.

Fearing that some tragedy might have befallen the rabbi, the congregants left the house of worship to look for him. Rabbi Salanter was not in his home. The streets and alleys also were searched in vain. As the people were about to give up hope of locating the rabbi, the sexton noticed a light burning in a window of a shack and he peered inside. To his amazement, he saw the saintly rabbi seated by the side of a cradle, rocking it gently.

Dashing into the shack, the sexton exclaimed: "Rabbi, the entire congregation is looking for you. The time for beginning the Kol Nidre service is already past. What are you doing here?"

Motioning to the sexton to be quiet, the rabbi softly rejoined: "On my way to the synagogue, long before sunset, I passed by this house and heard the crying of a baby. Receiving no reply when I knocked on the door, I entered and observed that the baby was alone. It was evident that the infant's mother had gone to the synagogue. So I remained here to rock the baby to sleep and to watch over him."

The Prophet Isaiah sums up the theme of Yom Kippur with these verses which are read during the Yom Kippur morning service:

> Is not this the fast that I have chosen?
> To loose the fetters of wickedness,
> To undo the bands of the yoke,
> And to let the oppressed go free. . . .
> Is it not to deal thy bread to the hungry
> And that thou bring the homeless to thy house?
> When thou seest the naked, that thou cover him,
> And that thou hide not thyself from thy fellow man.
> Then shall thy light break forth as the morning. . . .
> And thy righteousness shall go before thee.

The last of the five services that take up the entire day of Yom Kippur is the *Neilah* service. A most revealing story, which reaches its climax at *Neilah,* is told of an illiterate herdsman who dwelt in isolation throughout the year and came to the synagogue of the Baal Shem Tov on the Day of Atonement. Although the lad was unable to join the congregation in prayer, he grasped the significance and spirit of the occasion as the day wore on. He experienced a strong, urgent desire to participate with the congregation in pleading for atonement. As the *Neilah* service was drawing to a close, the herdsman removed from his pocket a reed whistle that he used while tending his flock and blew on it lustily.

The solemn sanctity of the *Neilah* prayers was disturbed and the chasidim angrily scolded the lad. However, the Baal Shem Tov in a calm, decisive voice, took his congregants to task: "Despite all your prayers, your learning and your piety, you haven't been able to prevail upon God to grant you pardon. This illiterate young herdsman, possessing a sincere desire to serve the Almighty, has opened the gates of repentance to all of us."

At the conclusion of the *Neilah* service, the Shofar is blown to signify the end of the fast; the end of the Day of Atonement.

chapter 11

THE PILGRIM FESTIVALS

The Jew is a master of many trades:

A matzoh baker on Passover.
A builder on Sukkot.
A gardener on Shavuot.
A Shofar blower on Rosh Hashanah.
A general on Lag B'Omer.
A Dreidel maker on Chanukah.
A Shalach Monot carrier on Purim.

THE BLESSING OF THY FESTIVALS!"

FESTIVAL PRAYER BOOK

THE PILGRIM FESTIVALS

Pesach, usually called Passover in English, is first in the calendar of Jewish festivals. For over two thousand years it has been more than a holiday; it has been *the* holiday, the festival of redemption; the festival of freedom. It commemorates the birth of a free nation, the Almighty's deliverance of Israel from slavery in Egypt through His messenger, Moses. The holiday begins on the evening of the 14th day of the Jewish month of Nisan.

Pharoah had been smitten nine times and had not yet consented to permit the Jews to leave Egypt. Just after midnight on the 14th day of Nisan, the tenth plague befell the Egyptians. Pharoah finally decided that he had had enough and ordered the Jews out of Egypt. The exodus, of course, was made in extreme haste and the Israelites had no time to prepare food. Even bread could not be made for there was no time to allow the dough to be leavened. So the emancipated slaves collected their dough before it was leavened and carried their kneading-troughs with them. Hastily, cakes made out of flour and water, called *matzoh,* were baked in the sun. Thus, on Pesach we eat *matzoh,* unleavened bread.

Tradition tells us that at midnight the Angel of Death visited the homes of the Egyptians, killing their first-born sons; but he *passed over* the houses of the Israelites and spared their first-born—which explains the name of the holiday. It has since become the custom for first-born Jewish sons to fast or attend a special service on the day preceding Passover, in appreciation of the Lord's sparing Israel's *b'chorim (first-born)*.

The festival features a pronouncement made during the Seder service: "In every generation man ought to regard himself as though he personally was freed from Egyptian bondage." We are asked to re-enact the Exodus as though it happened in our generation; to emphasize and re-emphasize the lessons of liberty that must remain fresh in the memory of mankind.

Passover lasts for seven days. The Sages added another day because of the inaccuracy of the calendar in ancient times. Not only is Passover known as *Zeman Cherutenu,* "Festival of Freedom," but also as *Chag Hamazot,* "Holiday of Matzot."

Although Pesach is one of the most popular of Jewish festivals, it is quite expensive to prepare for and involves a great deal of effort. Often, new utensils must be used. All dishes and food must be pure of anything that may be considered *chometz,* leaven. Of course, no *chometz* may be eaten or possessed during the holiday, so everything in the home must be entirely cleansed before Passover arrives.

The night before Pesach a ceremony known as *B'dikat Chometz,* searching out all leaven, is performed. Some crumbs of bread are put in noticeable places in every room. Then the head of the house, accompanied by another member of the household, searches every nook and corner with a lighted candle in his hand to make sure that no leaven has been left anywhere.

The *B'dikah* begins with the reciting of the benediction, "Blessed be Thou, O Lord our God, King of the universe, who hast sanctified us by Thy commandments, and hast commanded us concerning the precept of cleaning away the leaven." Then the crumbs that have been put out are gathered into a wooden spoon with a feather. On the following morning, after the last *chometz* meal, the remainder of the bread and the gathered crumbs on the spoon and the feather are burned. To disclaim ownership of any *chometz* which may be found unexpectedly during the forbidden period, the following prayer is recited: "All manner of

leaven that remains in my domain, which I have not seen or removed, shall be considered null and void, and accounted as the dust of the earth."

Since there may be *chometz* that can neither be eaten nor destroyed, it has become the custom to "sell the *chometz*" before Passover. At the present time, it is sold to the rabbi of the community, who, as agent, sells it in turn to a non-Jew. This is done by signing a document or by holding the end of a kerchief that the rabbi holds, an ancient traditional method of transferring ownership. The buyer, the non-Jew, keeps the bill of sale until the night after Passover, when he once again transfers ownership back to the rabbi, who in turn annuls his bill of sale. Thus the original owners have possession and title once again.

On the first two nights of Passover the *Seder* is celebrated. Seder means "order." The special readings, and ceremonies and meal of the evening are arranged according to a prescribed "order." The Seder ceremony is performed with great joy. Originally, it was designed to stimulate the interest of the Jewish child. In this regard, a charming custom developed. The children "steal" the *Afikomon*, a piece of matzoh which is put away at the beginning of the Seder, while the head of the family appears not to notice the theft. When the times comes to distribute the *Afikomon* (which means "dessert"), the master of the house offers a reward for its return so that the *Seder* meal may be properly ended.

The order of the *Seder* is as follows:

1. Pronounce the *Kiddush* for Passover over the first cup of wine.
2. Wash hands without reciting the blessing.
3. Eat any vegetable, usually radishes, cucumbers, onions or potatoes, dipped in salt water.
4. Split the middle matzoh into two halves, half of which is for the *Afikomon*.
5. Read the Haggadah.
6. Wash the hands and pronounce the proper blessing.
7. Pronounce the blessing over matzoh.

8. Eat *moror,* bitter herb, and *charoset,* a mixture of wine, apples and nuts, after saying the blessing.
9. Eat a sandwich of *moror.*
10. Eat the meal.
11. Recite Grace.
12. Complete the Haggadah.

A special *Seder* platter is set before the head of the household. The platter and table contain three *matzot,* bitter herbs, charoset, part of a chicken (wing or neck), an egg, salt water and the vegetable that is to be dipped in the salt water.

It is customary that each participant drink four cups of wine, because the Lord used four different expressions to Moses to indicate how He would free the Israelites from Egypt:

Vehotzeti	"And I will bring you out."
Vehitzalti	"And I will deliver you."
Vego-alti	"And I will redeem you."
Velokachti	"And I will take you out to Me for a people."

An extra cup of wine is especially prepared for the Prophet Elijah who, according to a legend, is supposed to visit every Jewish home on the *Seder* evening. This has given rise to the custom of opening the door a moment during the service in order that the expected prophet may enter as a most welcome guest.

The *Haggadah,* which is read during the *Seder* service, is really the story of the Jewish nation and an expression of its most profound aspirations. The children, as has been indicated before, are made an important part of the service and they actually start things off by asking the Four Questions. The Haggadah is recited in answer to the four questions.

Throughout the history of the Jews, *Pesach* has meant many things. However, the lasting message is suggested by the first of the Ten Commandments: "I am the Lord Thy God who brought thee out of the land of Egypt, out of the house of bondage." *Pesach,* in truth, marks the birth of a nation. Moses fashioned a nation out of a mass of slaves and gave them a faith. From that day on the Jews have never ceased to be a people with common

memories, problems, hopes and goals. Theirs was the first great mass emancipation. It set afire the imagination of mankind. It played a role in the American Revolution. It is interesting to note that on the American Liberty Bell, these words of Moses have been inscribed: "Proclaim liberty throughout the land to all the inhabitants thereof."

SHAVUOT: THE FEAST OF WEEKS

What is *Shavuot?* Actually, it is a Hebrew word meaning "weeks," and the holiday derives its name from the fact that it is celebrated exactly seven weeks after the second day of Passover, at the end of the *Sefira,* the counting of the *Omer.* Shavuot, the second of the three great Pilgrim festivals, is observed on the 6th and 7th day of Sivan. It commemorates the giving of the Torah to our people on Mount Sinai thousands of years ago.

Why did the Israelites receive the Torah seven weeks after their departure from Egypt? The Midrash relates an explanation given by Rabbi Itzchak: "The children of Israel should have received the Torah immediately upon departing from Egypt, but God said, 'My children have had no convalescence after their bondage in Egypt from which they have just been freed, and cannot receive the Torah so soon.'"

It wasn't so much the physical condition of the people that had to be considered, as their spiritual state. Hundreds of years of Egyptian bondage, being slaves to a people who had no feelings, no consideration for human beings, no true ethical teachings or morals, left a deep scar upon the Israelites which had to be healed before they could receive the holy Torah. The children of Israel were aware of this. They had been told that fifty days after their departure from Egypt they would receive the Torah, and they knew they had to make themselves worthy of that Divine gift. So they counted each day impatiently while they tried to better themselves, to improve their conduct and moral standards, to rise higher and higher as the time of the giving of the Torah drew closer.

God Himself helped them to better themselves, as He always does. God gave them a wonderful diet that was both physically and spiritually uplifting. He rained bread from heaven in the form of manna; He opened a fountain in the hard rock; He rained meat from the skies in the form of quails. He also showed them many other miracles and wonders. The children of Israel learned to recognize God; they saw that He could alter the course of nature for their sake. The last three days before the giving of the Torah were devoted to the most careful self-examination and preparation. When the great moment of the giving of the Torah finally came, the people were clean, pure and holy, in body and soul, and ready to receive the Torah. Unanimously they proclaimed: *Naaseh v'nishma!* "We shall do and obey."

Thus, Shavuot is called *Zeman Matan Toratenu*, Day of Giving of Our Law. Because it commemorates the giving of the Law, it is customary to spend the entire night of Shavuot studying the Law and a special book has been prepared for this occasion, called *Tikun Lel Shavuot*.

The two words, *naaseh v'nishma*, represent the formula of Torah Judaism. They form the cornerstone of our religious philosophy. Like trusted soldiers, the Jewish people have repeated *naaseh v'nishma* from generation to generation. Our mission has been to spread the Torah, the word of God, among the children of men. This is one reason why we are called the People of the Book.

Shavuot also marks the conclusion of the wheat festival. During the existence of the Temple at Jerusalem, the entire Jewish community brought a thanksgiving to the Almighty. It consisted of two loaves of bread baked of fine flour from the new crop of wheat. The sacrifice was accompanied by the singing of hymns by the Levites and the playing of harps and other musical instruments.

Dairy delicacies such as blintzes and cheese cake are eaten on Shavuot in honor of the Law of God, which is likened to "honey and milk." And the walls of the synagogue are decorated with greens and flowers.

The scroll containing the story of Ruth is read on Shavuot, too. This describes the harvesting in Israel and tells how Ruth embraced Judaism, so it is particularly appropriate.

157

Shavuot has been described by the Rabbis as the wedding day of God and Israel, the Torah being the marriage contract. As birthday and wedding day, Shavuot is indeed an outstanding occasion for rejoicing. Rashi said of Shavuot: "One should rejoice on it by eating and drinking to demonstrate that this day on which the Torah was given is acceptable to him."

SUKKOT: THE FEAST OF TABERNACLES

Unlike any other holiday, *Sukkot* is simply called *Z'man Simchatenu*, "Festival of Joy." Coming five days after Yom Kippur, it is a day of optimism because Jews are certain by then that God's verdict will be in their favor; solemnity is turned into solace and repentance into rejoicing.

Sukkot is associated with two principal ideas. First, it is a reminder of Israel's sojourn in the wilderness and the Lord's kind providence during that period. When our ancestors left Egypt, they wandered for forty years in the wilderness before they entered the Promised Land. During that time they were forced to live in *sukkot*, booths, or tabernacles. The Almighty, therefore, commanded the Jewish people throughout all generations to celebrate the Feast of Tabernacles. For seven days, from the 15th through the 21st day of the month of Tishri, they were to dwell in *sukkot*.

Second, Sukkot is the Jewish autumn festival of thanksgiving for the abundance of the harvest. The Jews of old observed it when they had finished the agricultural toil of the year. The seventh day of the holiday is known as *Hoshana Rabbah,* and is followed on the eighth day by a holiday called *Sh'mini Atzeret.* On the ninth day the gay holiday of *Simchat Torah* is observed. Each of these three days has its own special observance.

The entire family helps the father build and beautify the *sukkah*. It is made of wood or canvas or fiber board, and is decorated with fruits, vegetables, branches and flowers, testimony to the bounty of the Creator. During this festival the *sukkah* is considered as a temporary residence; all meals are served there and some pious Jews even sleep in it overnight.

158

The *sukkah* teaches us that there is no such thing as absolute security; man-made security is woefully uncertain. History has proven this to be true. True security comes from within. Thus, when a Jew enters his *sukkah* and recites the prayer that Providence "may spread over him the Tabernacle of His peace," and sits down with his family beneath the branch-covered roof through which the sky can be seen, he feels as though he is shielded by the Canopy of Divine Glory.

The mother, as well as the father, is represented in the *sukkah*. She lights the candles in the *sukkah* pronouncing the benedictions over them, and she also recites a special prayer for the occasion. On the table in the *sukkah* are two *chalot*, each shaped like a ladder.

To indicate their appreciation for the Lord's bounty, the Jews are commanded to take four species of plants:

> the *Etrog* (citron)
> the *Lulav* (branch of a palm tree)
> myrtle branches (*Hadassim*), and
> willows of the brook (*Aravot*).

and "rejoice before the Lord their God for seven days." Every morning during the first seven days of Sukkot, except on the Sabbath, before eating or drinking, the Jew takes his *Etrog* and *Lulav* and recites a benediction over them. This is done while standing and holding the Lulav in the right hand, the *Etrog* in the left. The benediction mentions the *Lulav* and not the *Etrog* or the other two species because the *Lulav* is the most prominent of the four species.

There are several interesting features in the Sukkot service. During the saying of *Hallel*, the *Lulav* is waved in six directions: South, North, East, upward, downward, and West. This symbolizes that the glory of the Lord surrounds and watches us from all sides. Later, the Holy Ark is opened and an ancient processional ceremony is enacted. The cantor goes first, then the rabbi, followed by all who have an *Etrog* and *Lulav*. They march around the entire synagogue as the cantor chants the *Hoshanah* prayer.

159

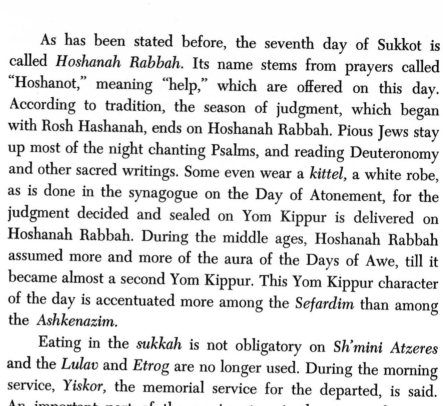

As has been stated before, the seventh day of Sukkot is called *Hoshanah Rabbah.* Its name stems from prayers called "Hoshanot," meaning "help," which are offered on this day. According to tradition, the season of judgment, which began with Rosh Hashanah, ends on Hoshanah Rabbah. Pious Jews stay up most of the night chanting Psalms, and reading Deuteronomy and other sacred writings. Some even wear a *kittel,* a white robe, as is done in the synagogue on the Day of Atonement, for the judgment decided and sealed on Yom Kippur is delivered on Hoshanah Rabbah. During the middle ages, Hoshanah Rabbah assumed more and more of the aura of the Days of Awe, till it became almost a second Yom Kippur. This Yom Kippur character of the day is accentuated more among the *Sefardim* than among the *Ashkenazim.*

Eating in the *sukkah* is not obligatory on *Sh'mini Atzeres* and the *Lulav* and *Etrog* are no longer used. During the morning service, *Yiskor,* the memorial service for the departed, is said. An important part of the service, too, is the prayer for rain, *Geshem.* Jews in every part of the world have prayed that God send rain in the ancient homeland of Israel at this season. The book of *Kohelet,* a philosophy on the vanity of life, is also read.

On the evening of the eighth day, Simchat Torah, the Rejoicing of the Law, gets under way. Men, women and children congregate in the synagogue, the children receive little flags made especially for this occasion, and everybody is in a jolly mood. There are processions, *Hakofot,* during which all the Scrolls from the Ark are carried by members of the congregation. The cantor, followed by the rabbi, leads the procession. The cantor chants as he marches, imploring the Almighty to help the Jewish people, and the verses are repeated by the congregation. At the end of each verse, when the procession reaches the starting point, the people break into joyful singing and dancing with the Torahs.

The next morning, the ninth day of Sukkot, there is again repeated the holiday merriment in the synagogue. This is preceded by reading the concluding chapters of the Torah and then proceeding to read from the first chapter of Genesis. Every male is called up to recite the blessing over the Torah and even the children under thirteen are given a group *aliya.* The picture is wonderful to behold. Children come forth from all sides and mount the platform from which the Torah is being read, ranging themselves in front of an older man who spreads his large *Talit* over their heads and pronounces the benediction. He recites it slowly, word by word, and the children repeat it after him, the entire congregation shouting "Amen" at the end with great fervor. Following this, the reading of the Torah is begun once more.

chapter 12

FEASTS, FASTS AND FESTIVALS

"Our ceremonialism is a training in self-
conquest while it links the generations . . .
and unifies our atoms dispersed to the four
corners of the earth as nothing else could."
Israel Zangwill

FEASTS, FASTS AND FESTIVALS

Chanukah, which lasts for eight days, from the 25th day of *Kislev* through the 2nd day of *Tevet*, is both a historical and a deeply spiritual holiday. It glorifies the Maccabean struggle for religious freedom and brings to mind a great miracle.

During the era of the Second Temple, when the Jews lived in the land of Judea, they were for a time under the domination of the ancient Greek kings. One of these kings, Antiochus IV, who ruled over Syria too, began a policy of persecution against the Jewish religion. He forbade the Jews to observe the Torah under the penalty of death. In addition, he forcibly took possesion of the Temple in Jerusalem and dedicated it to the Greek god Zeus. Oil usually kept in vessels sealed by the High Priest was made unusable for Temple purposes when it was defiled because of its use in the sacrifices offered to idols.

Not far from Jerusalem, in the quiet farming town of Modin, there lived the elderly and revered priest Mattathias and his five sons: Simon, Eliezer, Judah, Johanan and Jonathan. No longer able to stand the oppression of his people and the desecration of Judaism, Matthathias launched a rebellion one day by entering the market place and shouting, "Whoever is for the Lord, let him follow me!"

Before Mattathias died, he named his son Judah the Maccabee as his successor. A military genius, Judah organized bands that

166

were amazingly skillful at waging guerrilla warfare. All the odds were against them; they were ill-equipped and vastly outnumbered. But they knew the terrain, and they knew they were fighting for their homes, their faith and their freedom. They were imbued with the love of God, their people and their religion. They were determined not to forsake their teachings. They remembered that God has been on their side before in their battles against their enemies.

In the early winter of 165 B.C.E. the Jews defeated the demoralized armies of Antiochus. Judah marched victoriously into Jerusalem. His first act was to cleanse the Temple of its pollution. But when the priests went to light the menorah, they found only a single undefiled cruse of oil—one day's supply. Since throngs of Jews were waiting for the Temple ceremonies to begin, the priests had no choice but to use this single cruse of oil. Instead of lasting for one day, however, it burned for eight days and by then the priests had prepared fresh oil.

The dedication of the Temple took place on the 25th of Kislev. To commemorate this event and miracle of the oil, we celebrate Chanukah, which means "dedication," for eight days. Every man and woman observes the commandment of lighting the Chanukah Menorah and every child old enough, should be trained to light it. In some families only the head of the household lights the Menorah and pronounces the blessing, while all other members of the family gather around to say "Amen" and to sing *Mo'oz Tzur*, "Rock of Ages."

Because of the devotion of Hannah, who sacrificed her seven sons rather than allow them to bow down to the pagan god, the debt we owe to Jewish womanhood cannot be overlooked. The victory of Chanukah is a victory of the spirit as well as a victory over physical force because of the role of women like Hannah. Jewish survival throughout the ages has always been due, to a large extent, to the loyalty of Jewish women.

The story of Chanukah is fully recorded in the Book of Maccabees. Although we do not read this book at the synagogue service, the holiday is marked by special prayers of rejoicing for the miracle God wrought for His people, and homes are gladdened

167

with eight nights of celebration and gift giving. It is also customary to eat *latkes,* fried potato pancakes, on Chanukah.

The following three blessings are pronounced before lighting the Chanukah candles on the first evening. On the next seven nights, only the first two prayers are recited.

> Praised be Thou, O Lord our God, Ruler of the world, who hast sanctified us by Thy commandments, and hast bidden us to kindle the Chanukah lights.

> Praised be Thou, O Lord our God, Ruler of the world, who didst wondrous things for our fathers at this season in those days.

> Praised be Thou, O Lord our God, Ruler of the world, who hast granted us life, and hast sustained us to celebrate this joyous festival.

It is interesting to note that there was a dispute between the followers of Hillel and the disciples of Shammai over the order of lighting the candles. The latter advocated the lighting of eight on the first night and moving downward toward a single light on the last night. This may have reflected their basic view that the glory of Israel lay in the past. The House of Hillel, on the other hand, saw a glorious future for Judaism and advocated moving from a single light on the first night to a crescendo of eight lights on the last night. This is the accepted practice.

The Chanukah Menorah should be placed in a window which is visible from the street. If there is no window in the entire apartment facing the street, then it should be placed in a window in the back of the house which can be seen by the surrounding neighbors. For the festival of lights radiates a message of courage and hope to be shared with all mankind.

PURIM: FEAST OF LOTS

Purim is celebrated on the 14th and 15th days of Adar in memory of the deliverance of the Jews of Persia from their annihilation. Long ago, King Ahasueros was swayed by his wicked Prime Minister, Haman, to destroy all the Jews in his vast domain. Haman drew lots to decide the day on which to carry out this notorious massacre and the 14th of Adar was selected. Hence, this holiday is called Purim, the Feast of Lots.

Haman could surely never have imagined that his drawing of lots would some day furnish a name for the most joyous festival to be celebrated by the Jews. Purim is a time of dancing, masquerading, merrymaking, feasting and drinking. It is a day when *Hamantashen,* special little cakes filled with raisins, prunes or poppy seeds, are served. The *Hamantashen,* shaped like the three-cornered hats worn by ancient high officials, are symbolic of Haman's hat.

Tradition tells us that Haman rose from the position of a minor officer to one of high rank and power. Apparently he suffered from a deep inferiority complex and, in his fear of rivalry, forced everyone to kneel before him. But Mordecai dared to refuse. Haman was determined to make an example of him, especially since Mordecai was a Jew, a member of a defenseless people.

The story continues with the decree to kill all Jews. Things indeed looked black. But then Esther became Queen to King Ahasueros and she lost no time in uniting with Mordecai to foil the plot that Haman had conceived. King Ahasueros was finally convinced that Haman was evil and ordered him and his sons hung. The Jews of Persia were saved. In brief, this is the story read in *Megilat Esther,* the Book of Esther.

When the *Megilah* is read there is a great deal of activity in the synagogue. Every time Haman's name is mentioned, the children make noise with a noise-maker, called a *Greger* (or *Grogger*). The *Megilah* is read on the evening of the 13th day of the month of Adar, and again on the following morning.

The day of the 13th itself is observed as the Fast of Esther. Pious Jews do not eat or drink on this day, until after the evening reading of the Scroll of Esther. In the meantime, the women of the household busy themselves with the Purim feast. *Hamantaschen* are baked and other delicacies are prepared.

It is customary on Purim to send *Shalach Monot* to friends and neighbors. Generally, this consists of baskets containing

fruits, wines and confectionery. The children deliver these baskets and receive baskets in return for their parents. For in the book of Esther we read, "Therefore do the Jews . . . make the fourteenth day of the month Adar a day of gladness and feasting and of sending gifts to the poor."

The following day is known as *Shushan Purim* since in the capital of Persia, Shushan, the Jews celebrated Purim on the 15th of Adar.

CHAMISHA ASAR B'SHEVAT: JEWISH ARBOR DAY

In ancient Israel, Arbor Day was known as *Rosh Hashanah L'ilonot,* New Year for Trees. This holiday is generally celebrated by partaking of a variety of sweet fruits, especially Israeli fruits, such as figs, dates, raisins, almonds and grapes. A very special fruit eaten on this day is *Bokser,* St. John's bread.

Chamisha Asar B'Shevat, which means the 15th day of Shevat, was set aside in Palestine to promote and improve the planting of trees, especially those that bear fruits. Trees have played an especially important role in the rebuilding of Israel because of their shade, their fruit, their lumber and their usefulness in preventing soil erosion. The Israeli Government recently adopted a program of planting hundreds of thousands of trees in the Negev.

In Hebrew schools in this country special assemblies are held on Arbor Day, bags of fruit are given to the children, and children and grown ups alike buy Jewish National Fund tree certificates. In Israel the youngsters are given the privilege of planting new trees amidst a most impressive celebration.

ASARAH B'TEVET

The 10th day of the month of Tevet, *Asarah B'Tevet,* is a day of mourning; pious Jews neither eat nor drink until the stars become visible in the evening. For on this day in the year 586 B.C.E. King Nebuchadnezzar of Babylon laid siege to Jerusalem,

170

marking the beginning of the fall of the Kingdom of Judah and of the destruction of the First Temple, which had been built by King Solomon.

LAG B'OMER

Of the forty-nine days of the *Omer*, linking the two great festivals of Pesach and Shavuot, the thirty-third (lamed-gimel), always coinciding with the 18th of Iyar, stands out with a significance of its own. It is the only cheerful day in the *Sefirah* period when all rules of mourning are suspended.

Lag B'Omer is associated with two great names in Jewish History, Rabbi Akiba and his chief disciple, Rabbi Shimon ben Jochai. Rabbi Akiba was a great supporter of the revolution that Bar Kochba led against the Romans, and it was during this revolution that a dreadful plague broke out among Rabbi Akiba's students. Many of them died. On Lag B'Omer the epidemic suddenly stopped. Our Sages therefore ordered that this day be observed as a semi-holiday. For this reason, Lag B'Omer has become known as the Scholar's Festival. It is celebrated by Hebrew School students who, together with their teachers, go into the fields to study and engage in mock battle.

Rabbi Shimon ben Jochai defied a Roman decree against Torah study and continued to instruct his students in the Law of God. This he bravely did even though he was aware that his teacher and many other scholars had been tortured to death for defying the very same law.

For a dozen years Shimon ben Jochai lived with his son Rabbi Eleazar in a mountain cave. They did not leave the cave because they feared discovery by Roman spies. Through a miracle, a spring of water miraculously appeared in the cavern to provide them with drink. A carob tree grew in the cave and provided father and son with fruit. In order to preserve their garments, they sat naked in the sand and their skin became covered with scabs. They left their cave when they learned that the Roman Emperor had died. Some pious Jews believe that ben Jochai died on Lag B'Omer, and that before he passed on he revealed to

his pupils the secrets which were later incorporated in the Zohar.

There are many stories that can be read about the bravery of Bar Kochba, who was one of the great heroes of Jewish history and who made a last effort to free the Jews from the tyranny of Rome.

SHIVAH ASAR B'TAMMUZ

It was on *Shivah Asar B'Tammuz*, the 17th day of the month of Tammuz, in the time of the Second Temple, that the Romans broke into Jerusalem. Our Rabbis considered the destruction of the Second Temple a great national calamity, in fact greater than the destruction of the First Temple. Thus, the Prophets and later the sages, decreed that a fast be observed on the day the Romans penetrated the walls of Jerusalem, for this enabled them to destroy the Temple three weeks later.

TISHAH B'AV

The three week period from *Shivah Asar B'Tammuz* to *Tishah B'Av*, the 9th day of the month of Av, is one of mourning in remembrance of the terrible misfortunes that befell the Jews at this time many centuries ago. During this period the Jews observe some of the rules that apply to those who mourn the death of a relative. No marriages are performed, no new garments are purchased, and even hair cuts are not permitted. From the 1st to the 9th of Av, the grief of the Jews grows deeper and they observe even more stringent rules of mourning to express their deep sorrow at the approaching day of doom.

Tishah B'Av, the day on which the Babylonians destroyed the First Temple and the Romans the Second Temple, is a fast day. All the rules of mourning are observed.

On the evening of the 8th of Av, the Jew goes to synagogue to listen to the somber chanting of Lamentations. This is one of the books of the Bible written by the Prophet Jeremiah, who lived during the destruction of the First Temple. In many synagogues shoes must be removed if they are made of leather, as during mourning, and congregants sit either on low stools or the floor. When the service ends the usual greetings are not offered, nor are they exchanged upon returning home. Sadness reigns.

Even the *talit* and *tefillin* are not worn on Tishah B'Av morning because they are considered holy vestments. In the synagogue, the Jew once again sits on the floor as he listens to the reading of Lamentations. When the morning prayers are over, the Jew again does not greet anyone either in the synagogue or on his way home.

The fast lasts all day, until after the appearance of the stars. The *talit* and *tefillin* are put on during Mincha.

The Sabbath following the first nine days of Av is called *Sabbath Nachamu*, the Sabbath of Comfort. It takes its name from the fortieth chapter of Isaiah which is read as the Haftorah and begins with the words, *Nachamu, Nachamu,* "comfort ye, comfort ye." With these words, the Jew once again has confidence that God will help him and that justice and truth will finally triumph.

chapter 13

ISRAEL RETURNS

The Lord shall set his hand a second time
to recover the remnants of His people. . . .
And He shall set up an ensign for the nations and shall assemble the outcast of
Israel and gather together the depressed
of Judah from the four corners of the
earth.

Isaiah 11: 11, 12

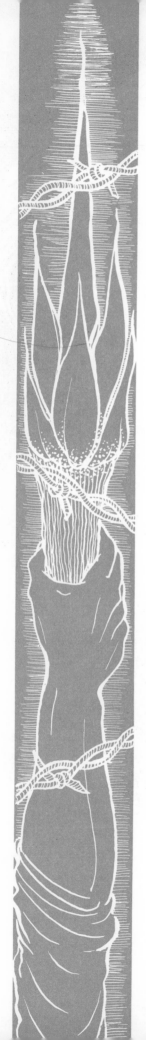

ISRAEL RETURNS

Israel Becomes Jewish State!" On May 15, 1948 this newspaper headline electrified Jews everywhere and marked a new world-wide Jewish holiday: *Yom Atzmaut,* Israel Independence Day. After almost twenty centuries of prayers, hard work and bitter fighting, a Jewish government was restored in the Promised Land; an ancient dream come true. In accordance with the United Nations decision of November 29, 1947, the Jew was free to turn the shifting sands and swampy wastelands into fertile valleys and blossoming orchards.

Just where is Israel? This tiny democracy lies at the cross-walks of the world and connects three continents, Europe, Asia and Africa. It is so small you can drive across it in less than a day. Its width runs from 20 to 70 miles, and it stretches along the Mediterranean for only 150 miles. Still, Israel has almost everything: mountains, plateaus, plains, valleys, desolate deserts, lakes and an extended coastline. From the Dead Sea, 1,292 feet below sea-level, it rises to the hills of Galilee, 4,000 feet above sea-level. This is the land that was given to the Jews by God. In the Book of Genesis we read:

> The word of the Lord came unto Abram . . .
> And He said unto him:
> 'I am the Lord that brought thee out of Ur of the
> Chaldees, to give thee this land to inherit it. . . .'

178

In that day the Lord made a covenant with Abram, saying: 'Unto thy seed have I given this land, from the river of Egypt unto the great river, the river Euphrates.'

Further on in Genesis God declares:

"And I will give unto thee, and to thy seed after thee, the land of thy sojournings, all the land of Canaan, for an everlasting possession. . . ."

After the long journey from Egypt, Joshua, with Divine blessing, led the people across the Jordan to settle in the Promised Land. The Hebrews prospered, worked hard and were devoted to the soil. At first, they were governed by Judges. Then, at their behest, the Prophet Samuel anointed Saul the first King of the Hebrews. This Kingdom lasted less than two centuries. Aggression, bloodshed and destruction followed.

The Assyrians descended upon the Israelites and carried away 27,000 prisoners. Later, Nebuchadnezzar led a Babylonian Army which defeated the Assyrians and reduced the city of Jerusalem, including the Temple, to rubble. Before fifty years had passed the Babylonians were conquered by the Persians, who permitted the Jews to return home. Under the inspiration of the Prophets Haggai and Zechariah the Second Temple was built.

But the Holy Land became a battleground for the major powers of these days and in the period that followed it changed hands twenty-two times. Ninety years after the Maccabees recaptured the Temple, the Roman general Pompey marched into Jerusalem, slaughtered the Jews and annexed the land to the Roman Empire. In the year 70, Jerusalem fell to Titus; perhaps a million persons died in combat or starved to death. The Temple was reduced to ashes and the city left in ruins. Bar Kochba, inspired by the great Rabbi Akiba, attempted to oust the Roman legions. Though he won some telling victories, he was finally defeated.

In 614, the Persians captured Palestine. In 636, the ancient homeland of the Jews became part of the vast domain of Islam. Turkey was next in line to conquer Palestine. In 1099, the

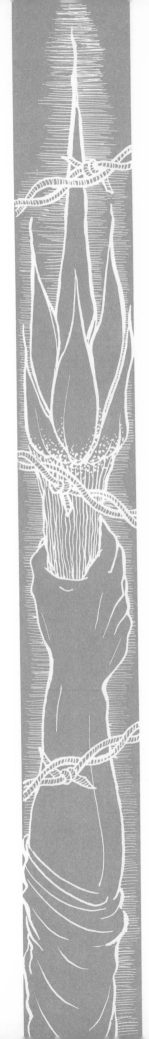

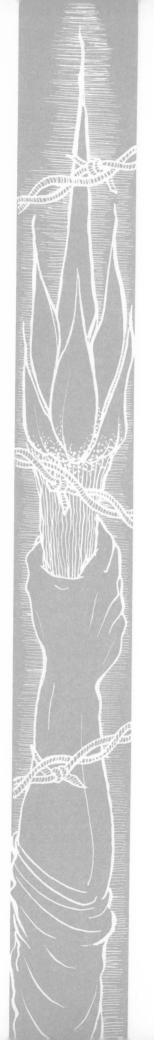

Crusaders captured Jerusalem and slaughtered Jews and Moslems alike. From 1291 to 1561, Palestine was a province of Egypt.

Throughout the following centuries foreign powers continued to manifest interest in the Holy Land. Napoleon invaded Palestine in 1799. From 1840 on the Turkish Government strengthened its hold on Palestine. This rule ended when the Turks were defeated in World War I. From 1918 to the rebirth of the Jewish State in 1948, the British governed Palestine.

On November 2, 1917, Lord Arthur James Balfour, Britain's Secretary for Foreign Affairs, issued the famous Balfour Declaration. It said: "His Majesty's Government views with favor the establishment of a national home for the Jewish people in Palestine, and will use their best endeavors to facilitate the achievement of this objective."

Jews throughout the world greeted this pronouncement with great enthusiasm. With the British certain to take over rule of the area, they felt a Jewish homeland in Palestine was now more than a mere dream. Though driven from his land centuries ago, the Jew never gave up his love for it. He transplanted the Holy Land into his very heart. He sang of Palestine and dreamed of Palestine; mourned for Palestine and hoped for Palestine. Pagan, Christian, Mohammedan, Roman, Egyptian, Turk . . . all had conquered the land, but none was able to make it his own. The land never prospered. As Zangwill said, "The land without a people waited for the people without a land."

This love and attachment of the Jew to Eretz Israel was a living example of loyalty. Every Jewish celebration took into account the loss of the Temple and Israel. A bag of soil from Israel was considered a most precious possession. *Sukkot* was celebrated with an *Etrog* imported from the Holy Land. *Kiddush* was chanted over wine pressed from grapes of the vineyards of their forefathers. Three times a day the return to the ancient homeland was prayed for. The Jews knew that the most distinguished sages "were wont to kiss the boundaries of Eretz Israel, kiss its stones and linger in its dust, fulfilling the words of the Psalmist: 'For Thy servants take pleasure in her stones, and favor the dust thereof.'" In his poem, "Longing for Jerusalem," Judah Halevi writes:

180

"O City of the world, with sacred splendor blest,
My spirit yearns to thee from out the far-off West,
A stream of love wells forth when I recall thy day,
Now is thy Temple waste, thy glory passed away.
Had I an eagle's wings, straight would I fly to thee,
Moisten thy holy dust with wet cheeks streaming free."

And so, Friday May 14, 1948, corresponding to the 5th of Iyar 5708, was a day of decision. The next day the British Mandate would expire and the soldiers of the Empire would leave. The Jews had to be ready. The members of the National Council met in Tel Aviv. A great deal had to be done. It was *Erev Shabbat*, and the signing of the Declaration of Independence had to be completed before sundown.

As the meeting began, seven Arab countries—Iraq, Syria, Lebanon, Trans-Jordan, Saudi Arabia, Yemen, Egypt—declared war against the infant Jewish State. Heavily mechanized columns of the Arab Legion attacked Jewish settlements. The Egyptian army moved in on the colonies of the Negev. Tel Aviv was bombed! Israel's soldiers were greatly outnumbered and poorly equipped, lacking even a single fighter-plane, but they had faith and determination; they would never again permit a foreign government to dominate their God-given country.

To the thundering of cannons and the rhythm of marching soldiers, David Ben Gurion rose from his seat. Flanked by the twelve members of the Council, his unruly white hair floating like a halo around his head, he slowly read aloud Israel's Declaration of Independence:

The land of Israel was the birthplace of the Jewish people. Here, their spiritual, religious and national identity was formed. Here, they achieved independence and created a culture of national and universal significance. Here, they wrote and gave the Bible to the world.

Exiled from Palestine, the Jewish people remained faithful to it in all the countries of the dispersion, never ceasing to pray and hope for their return and for the restoration of their national freedom.

181

Impelled by this historic association, Jews strove throughout the centuries to go back to the land of their fathers and regain statehood. In recent decades they returned in great numbers. They reclaimed a wilderness, revived their language, built cities and villages and established a vigorous and ever-growing community, with its own economic and cultural life. They sought peace, yet were ever prepared to defend themselves. They brought the blessing of progress to all the inhabitants of the country.

In the year 1897, the first Zionist Congress, inspired by the vision of Theodor Herzl of a Jewish State, proclaimed the right of the Jewish people to a national revival in their own country.

This right was acknowledged by the Balfour Declaration of November 2, 1917, and reaffirmed by the mandate of the League of Nations, which gave explicit international recognition to the historic connection of the Jewish people with Palestine and their right to reconstitute their national home.

The Nazi holocaust which engulfed millions of Jews in Europe proved anew the urgency of the re-establishment of the Jewish State, which would solve the problem of Jewish homelessness by opening the gates to all Jews and lifting the Jewish people to the status of equality in the family of nations.

Survivors of the European catastrophe as well as Jews from other lands, claiming their right to a life of dignity, freedom and labor, and undeterred by hazards, hardships and obstacles, tried unceasingly to enter Palestine.

During the Second World War, the Jewish people in Palestine made a full contribution in the struggle of freedom-loving nations against the Nazi evil. The sacrifices of their soldiers and the efforts of their workers gained them title to rank with the peoples who founded the United Nations. On November 29, 1947, the General Assembly of the United Nations adopted a resolution for the re-establishment of an independent Jewish State in Palestine and called upon the inhabitants of the country to take such steps as may be necessary on their part to put the plan into effect.

This recognition by the United Nations of the rights of the Jewish people to establish their independent state may not be revoked. It is, moreover, the self-evident right of the Jewish people to be a nation, as all other nations, in its own sovereign State.

Accordingly we, the members of the National Council, representing the Jewish people in Palestine and the Zionist movement of the world, meeting together in solemn assembly by virtue of the natural and historic right of the Jewish people and the resolution of the General Assembly of the United Nations, DO HEREBY PROCLAIM THE ESTABLISH-MENT OF A JEWISH STATE IN PALESTINE, TO BE CALLED ISRAEL.

We hereby declare that as of the termination of the man-date at midnight, this night of the 14th to 15th of May 1948, and until the setting up of duly elected bodies of the State in accordance with a constitution to be drawn up by a Constituent Assembly not later than the 1st day of October, 1948, the present National Council shall act as the Provisional State Council. Its executive organ, the National Administra-tion, shall constitute the Provisional Government of the State of Israel.

The State of Israel will promote the development of the country for the benefit of all its inhabitants; will be based on precepts of liberty, justice and peace taught by the Hebrew Prophets; will uphold the full social and political equality of all its citizens without distinction of race, creed or sex; will guarantee full freedom of conscience, worship, education and culture; will safeguard the sanctity and in-violability of shrines and holy places of all religions, and will dedicate itself to the principles of the United Nations.

The State of Israel will be ready to cooperate with the organs and representatives of the United Nations in the implementation of the Resolution of November 29, 1947, and

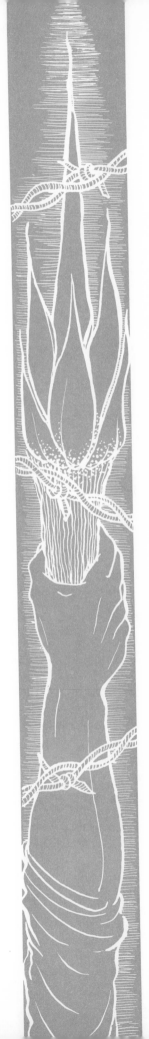

will take steps to bring about an economic union over the whole of Palestine.

We appeal to the United Nations to assist the Jewish people in the building of its state and to admit Israel into the family of Nations.

In the midst of the wanton aggression heaped upon us these many months, we call upon the Arab inhabitants of the State of Israel to return to the ways of peace and play their part in the development of the State, with full and equal citizenship and due representation in all its bodies and institutions, provisional or permanent.

We offer peace and amity to all neighboring States and their peoples, and invite them to cooperate with the independent Jewish nation for the common good of all. The State of Israel is ready to contribute its full share to the peaceful progress and reconstruction of the Middle East. Our call goes out to the Jewish people all over the world to rally to our side in the task of immigration and development, and to stand by us in the great struggle for the fulfillment of the dream of generations, the redemption of Israel.

With trust in Almighty God, we set our hand to this declaration, at this Session of the Provisional State Council, in the city of Tel Aviv, on this Erev Shabbat, the fifth of Iyar, 5708, the fourteenth day of May, 1948.

When Ben Gurion finished reading the declaration (it took seventeen minutes) many of the people were weeping. Everyone rose and sang *Hatikvah*, the song that had been adopted as the Jewish National Anthem by the First Zionist Congress. Then the ancient benediction was chanted:

> "Blessed art Thou, O Lord our God, King of the universe, who has kept us in life and preserved us and enabled us to reach this season."

Finally, with obvious emotion, the members of the Council signed the Declaration.

The president of the most influential country on earth lost no time in providing great encouragement and moral support to the newly established state.

A PRESIDENT OF THE UNITED STATES SPEAKS ON ISRAEL

One of the proudest moments of my life occurred at 6:12 p.m. on Friday, May 14 (1948) when I was able to announce recognition of the new State of Israel by the Government of the United States. In view of the long friendship of the American people for the Zionist ideal it was particularly appropriate that our Government should be the first to recognize the new State.

Harry S. Truman

No country ever had a more difficult birth. Israel was attacked from all directions. It was outnumbered forty to one, and Arab units such as the British trained Arab Legion had modern weapons and unlimited military resources. Abdul Rahman Azzam Pasha, Secretary General of the Arab League declared: "This war will be a war of extermination and a momentous massacre which will be spoken of like the Mongol Massacres and the Crusades."

The tiny but well-trained Haganah became the Israel Defense Army. Small squads of Jewish soldiers went out to meet the invading enemy hoards. With discarded, surplus weapons from other countries, they miraculously beat back the weakly motivated Arabs while the world looked on in amazement. Only the old city of Jerusalem fell into enemy hands, and this too could have been recaptured had not the United Nations declared a truce at the very time the Israeli Army was launching a counter-attack on the ancient walled section of Jerusalem.

The Jewish soldier, remembering the promise that the Almighty had made to Abraham, "Unto you I shall give the land and unto your children after you," could not be vanquished. What he lacked in modern arms and supplies he made up for with faith and determination, with an unequalled spirit sparked

185

by his knowledge of the Bible and the wisdom of the Sages. His motto, derived from the Bible was always:

> "If I forget thee, O Jerusalem, let my right hand forget her cunning. Let my tongue cleave to the roof of my mouth if I remember thee not. . . ."

On June 11, the siege of New Jerusalem was broken. Count Folke Bernadotte, the U. N. mediator, ordered a four-week truce. Though this armistice was accepted by Israel, the Egyptian Army continued attacking Jewish settlements in the Negev and dropping bombs on Tel Aviv.

The Israeli Army was dispatched to the Negev. Within ten days it captured Beersheba, the strategic gateway to the Southern Desert. Soon separate truce agreements were signed with Lebanon, Trans-Jordan and Syria. The war was over. The tiny State of Israel had triumphed over its enemies. The lamp that had been extinguished for nearly 2,000 years was again relit. A miracle had occurred.

Thus, the Israelis proved a statement that had been made earlier in the year: "Right is on our side. With us are the hopes of the past generations of our people. With us is the conscience of the world. With us are deposited the testament of the millions of our martyred dead and the resolute will to live of the millions who have survived. The sanctity of our martyrs and heroes rests upon us, and the God of our fathers will help us."

God indeed had helped. Jeremiah had prophesied correctly: "And I will gather you from all the nations, and from all the places whither I have driven you," saith the Lord, "and I will bring you back unto the place whence I caused you to be carried away captive."

Today Israel's flag flies over the United Nations. Today Israel's ambassadors are received in the capitals of the world. As David Ben Gurion has said: "This country made us a people, and our people made this country."

186

But, above all, the third return of the Jews to the Promised Land must make all of us everywhere hear more clearly the message of Sinai:

"And thou shalt love the Lord thy God with all thy heart and all thy soul and all thy might."

For it is the voice of the Almighty, the Torah, which has been responsible for the survival of the Jews over the centuries in the face of all adversity.

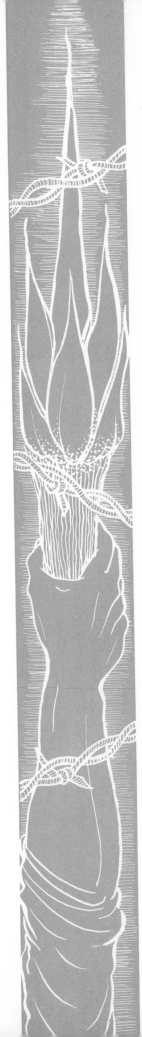

EPILOGUE

The purpose of this book has been to provide you, the Jewish teen-ager, with renewed appreciation for the inspiring Jewish heritage that is our cherished possession. This rich past that is ours also contains within it the power to provide each of us with the promise for a rich future.

Our primary goal is to achieve a full and happy life as Americans and as Jews. We can achieve this by remaining loyal to the goals of American democracy without compromising our loyalty to Judaism.

The famous humorist, Sam Levenson, has given much thought to this subject and recently expressed his "Jewish Credo" in these words:

"I am a happy Jew, free and well-adjusted: I have cured myself of possible Jewish schizophrenia (a common disease) through identification with my people. I have found that the more deeply I become identified with the values of my own people, the closer do I come to an understanding of the hopes and desires of mankind as a whole.

"When in my TV performances I draw from the folklore of my own people—for example, Mama's attitude toward family, children, home, God—I am invariably flooded with mail from non-Jews who ask, 'What makes you think your mother was different? My mother used to be the same way.'

"I am always conscious that I am a Jew. I always carry the responsibility of being a Jew. I tell no dialect jokes, no stories that could be offensive to a minority group, no "little Jew" stories. There were no "little Jews" in the fight for Israel's independence, there were no "little Jews" in the Warsaw ghetto, there were no "little Jews" in Okinawa.

"There are Jews in my profession who have suggested that I change my name. "You can get much farther that way," they say. True. You can get farther, farther and farther. But how far away do I care to go? And if I am not accepted as a Jew, but as a "Neutral," what have I achieved?"

A voice calls out to each of us to express his credo, for we can not be "neutral" about Judaism or about life.

And now that you are a full-fledged member in Israel, now that you are a Bar Mitzvah or a daughter in Israel, that voice calls to you. Study the traditions of your people and live by them proudly, so that your children may learn them too. Only in this way can the survival of Israel be guaranteed. As we said in the very first chapter of this book, the future of the Jewish people is now in your hands. Your own future is also in your hands. Whether you will continue to be an active, educated, well-adjusted happy Jew is up to you!